＃ 30- 2001

P9-DGV-603

5381
.8542
2000

Outdoor Careers
2nd Edition

Exploring Occupations in
Outdoor Fields

SOUTHEASTERN COMMUNITY
COLLEGE LIBRARY
WHITEVILLE, NC 28472

by Ellen Shenk

STACKPOLE
BOOKS

0 11557 02873 7

Copyright © 1992, 2000 by Stackpole Books

Published by
Stackpole Books
5067 Ritter Road
Mechanicsburg, PA 17055
www.stackpolebooks.com

All rights reserved, including the right to reproduce this book or portions thereof in any form or by any means, electronic or mechanical, including photocopying, recording, or by any information storage and retrieval system, without permission in writing from the publisher. All inquiries should be addressed to Stackpole Books, 5067 Ritter Road, Mechanicsburg, Pennsylvania 17055.

Printed in the United States of America

Cover design by Wendy A. Reynolds
Cover photos by Paul Rezendes

10 9 8 7 6 5 4 3 2

Second Edition

Library of Congress Cataloging-in-Publication Data

Shenk, Ellen.
    Outdoor careers: exploring occupations in outdoor fields/Ellen Shenk.
        —Rev. ed.
        p. cm.
    Includes bibliographical references and index.
    ISBN 0-8117-2873-0 (alk. paper)
        1. Vocational guidance. 2. Occupations. 3. Outdoor life—Vocational guidance. 4. Outdoor recreation—Vocational guidance. I. Title.

HF5381 .S542 2000
331.7'02—dc21

                                                                        99-047776

Contents

Foreword

The media are filled with stories of urban sprawl, of sedentary citizens of all ages who sit glued to the couch in front of a TV, and of many who seemingly seldom open their doors thanks to an Internet that meets much of their demands.

Yet, if the truth be known, for most of us, a highlight of our day is the time we get outside. How often have you heard someone say, "It feels so good to be outside. Just feel that fresh air." Ask a class of third graders what they plan to look for when they select a career, and right up near the top will be "something that lets me work outside."

Many people, some profiled in this fine book, have jobs that allow them to combine the benefits of nature with a successful career. Far more people, I am sure, would enjoy an outdoor occupation if they simply knew more about how to find those careers. Others assume that the only careers that offer a comfortable living are found within the confines of an office, factory, or store.

That there are many fine careers that offer outdoor work has been proved by author Ellen Shenk, in this revision of her popular book. I'm delighted that the response to her earlier volume encouraged the development of this revised and expanded sequel.

Her book details the practical side of outdoor work, rather than just an insipid "Wouldn't it be great if I could work outdoors?" It describes some real and interesting careers involving outdoor work. To prove the point, it cites the lives of a number of successful practitioners of outdoor jobs. Fringe benefits of many of these careers include the opportunity to teach others, to protect our environment, and to directly contribute to the happiness and well-being of those around us.

The author, a friend of a dozen years and an esteemed professional colleague, enjoys a well-deserved reputation for careful investigation, sound research, and clear writing. I am particularly pleased that the author, who worked for a number of years in the career field in Canada, included information on careers north of the border.

An occasional newspaper feature will profile a former Wall Street broker, an Atlanta accountant, or a San Francisco lawyer who walked away from an urban lifestyle to find greater happiness working outdoors—perhaps as a park administrator, a summer camp director, or an organic farmer. But their stories are only the tip of the iceberg, and the author has discovered dozens of careers for both former urbanites and those beginning their job search for the first time.

That widely quoted man of letters Mark Twain once said something like "The luckiest people in the world work year-round at what they would normally elect to do during summer vacation." Many of those described on these pages did indeed begin their outdoor careers by building on something they found they liked during a vacation or while pursuing a hobby.

I hope that you, like them, may find in these pages clues to what may be a satisfying and fulfilling outdoor career for you.

Robert Calvert, Jr.
Editor, Career Opportunities News

Acknowledgments

In the process of updating this book I received assistance from many people. I am extremely grateful for the librarians in the Fairfax County, Virginia, library system, who were unfailingly helpful and courteous anytime I asked their assistance. People in various careers shared information and perspectives on their daily work; many others from organizations across the country sent helpful materials and answered my questions.

I especially thank Marlene Bryan, career counselor, who reviewed the career and job-search sections; Nancy Brooks, publications specialist extraordinaire, for her organizational, research, and sounding board functions; and my editor, Mark Allison, who gave opinions when asked but mainly let me do the work. Above all, I give special thanks to my family and friends. Their understanding, support, and encouragement were essential in helping me complete this project.

Introduction

"There is a presence and an influence in Nature and the Open which expands the mind and causes brigand cares and worries to drop off—whereas in confined places foolish and futile thoughts of all kinds swarm the microbes and cloud and conceal the soul."

Edward Carpenter

The lure of the outdoors and of work in the outdoors is a great attraction for many people. This book is addressed to those of you who are interested in the outdoors and want a career that reflects that interest. All of the careers covered relate in some way to the outdoors, either involving a significant amount of work outside or building on outdoor interests.

Two of the words used in this book must be clarified. The term *outdoors* is used as defined by Webster: "out of doors; in the open air." The use of the word *career* follows another Webster definition: "profession." *Career, occupation,* and *job* are used interchangeably today and throughout this book. Because *career* is now receiving the widest usage, it has been selected for the book title.

This book will introduce the major areas of outdoor work and provide information about a number of careers available in each one. It is intended to make you aware of the many options and opportunities and to help give you direction in choosing a career.

HOW TO USE THIS BOOK

This book was first published in 1992. The copy you hold in your hands is a revised and enlarged edition. In this edition, every effort has been made to accurately update data about pay and outlook for every career covered. Additional careers have been added, and the resources sections in each chapter, which point to further information on the career or topic of the chapter, have been enlarged. Internet addresses for organizations cited or for jobs listings have also been included in this edition.

Canadian resources have been added to this edition. Many of the organizations that provide career information have members in both Canada and the United States and the career information they give is applicable for both countries. Where I could obtain listings of Canadian organizations and information about Canadian government jobs, however, they have been added to make the data in this book as helpful as possible to all readers.

Related careers are grouped in chapters under general headings. The careers are also listed in the index by title. If you are looking for a specific occupation and want to find it quickly, check the index. Reading the whole book, however, may open up additional options you hadn't previously considered, so don't be too hasty in zeroing in on specific information.

Persons in various professions have been profiled to put a human face on the career descriptions and give a glimpse of how different people feel about their work. Reading about how these persons have found their way and what they do, along with their advice, should give you ideas and information to aid your search for a career that fits your special interests and abilities.

The book also includes critical information about the process of choosing a career and conducting a job search. Selecting a career and the job search have been the focus of entire books, however, and you may wish to research further using the suggested books.

One caution: Be aware of the limitations of the printed page. Every effort has been made to obtain up-to-date information for this book, but careers respond very quickly to changing economic conditions. In a volatile economic climate, career information is subject to change, particularly regarding salaries and the availability of positions.

Additionally, salaries vary widely depending on the size and type of employer and on local economic conditions. Although all attempts have been made to obtain accurate salary figures, there will be variations between localities. The figures are given to provide you with an idea of what the salary range may be. Use this book as a guide, not the authoritative word.

A book of this size cannot pretend to be the last word on the subject of outdoor work. It is intended to be a starting point, not the final destination. But it should expand your horizons, help focus your career search, and give you ideas of where to go for additional information.

SEASONAL OUTDOOR WORK

Many people are able to find satisfactory full-time employment in outdoor careers by creatively combining several career options. The conservation and recreation fields offer many part-time or seasonal jobs. The chapters on these areas give some information about seasonal work and list specific resources. Part-time positions do exist in other fields, however, so anyone looking for an outdoor career should consider the possibility of utilizing part-time work in the search for a perfect job fit.

Bob Birkby, who is profiled in chapter 9, has found writing to be complementary to rigorous summer outdoor positions. From his own experience, Birkby offers some advice for persons looking for outdoor work: "People interested in full-time outdoor careers have a tough challenge ahead. The agencies [such as the National Park Service and U.S. Forest Service] don't have many openings these days, and their hiring guidelines cause opportunities to be even more limited.

"Seasonal outdoor work is much more accessible, and it allows people to build up experience that can make them more qualified for full-time employment. Some mountaineers I've worked with went through NOLS [National Outdoor Leadership School] training, and then became NOLS instructors before forming their own company. The Student Conservation Association hires over a hundred supervisors each summer for its Conservation Work Crew program, and it places close to a thousand volunteers in twelve-week resource assistant internships with agencies all over America.

"Having a special skill can make a person much more marketable. In my case, my trail construction expertise has opened lots of doors. During the summers I spent at Philmont [a Boy Scout camp in New Mexico] learning trail work, I earned barely enough to cover my expenses, but I think that's going to be the case when learning most outdoor skills. Lots of people want to do this sort of thing, and many are willing to do anything for a while to make it happen. That means the entry-level and apprenticeship positions don't pay much, and until a person has some significant experience under his or her belt, moving beyond those temporary, low-paying jobs is not very easy."

Several organizations offer training or some positions in outdoor or wilderness skills. The National Outdoor Leadership School teaches wilderness skills and leadership with emphasis on conservation and ethics. It also holds educational conferences and seminars and does publishing and research on wilderness-related topics. Outward Bound is an educational program that uses challenging wilderness activities to train for leadership and assist with self-discovery. It operates several schools throughout the country and has about one thousand seasonal employees and fewer than two hundred full-time employees.

The Appalachian Mountain Club offers a variety of employment opportunities in trail work, education, facilities and hotel management, and other related fields. The Student Conservation Association gives opportunities for high school and adult volunteers to work on conservation projects across the country. This provides some jobs for both leading the volunteers and exposing them to a variety of conservation careers. Addresses for these four organizations are listed in the Resources section at the end of this introduction.

ADDITIONAL OUTDOOR FIELDS

The scope of this book does not allow for coverage of all occupations that involve work in the outdoors. Some, such as military careers, were deliberately omitted. Although all branches of the military offer varied jobs in the outdoors, they are not included in this book because the ultimate choice of job assignment belongs with the military, not with the individual.

Law enforcement is another career that, depending upon the type of job and the location, offers a fair amount of work outdoors in all types of weather. Increasingly, law enforcement positions are available in the National Parks, as mentioned in chapter 4. Many people find that this work offers rewards that include helping others and satisfaction because the work is so important. Reasons for choosing careers in law enforcement seldom include working in the outdoors, however.

Anthropology is another field that usually involves some work in the outdoors. A social science, anthropology examines the origins, the physical development, and the cultures of human beings. Although anthropologists work in universities, colleges, and museums, most also do field work in places as diverse as the Arctic and Africa. Linguistic anthropologists, who study the development of languages, may spend time visiting tribes that have no written languages. Cultural anthropologists often study groups or tribes of people; they conduct their research by interviewing people and observing their behavior.

Archaeology, a subfield of anthropology, studies human societies by examining articles such as tools, art, artifacts, and utensils. Archaeologists go to locations that housed early cities, cemeteries, or dumping grounds to study. They often spend long hours sifting painstakingly through sand or soil, sometimes in remote locations with crude living conditions.

Additional outdoor careers that are not covered in the book are careers that provide vicarious recreation for others: the sports careers. Professional sports such as football, baseball, and tennis are, indeed, outdoor careers. But they have been deliberately omitted from this book under the assumption that few individuals would pick up this book, read about one of those careers, and decide to pursue that career. Another sporting career, professional bull rider, was recently cited in a career publication as one of the most rapidly growing sports in the U.S. The pay for this work, which is extremely physical with great potential for injuries, ranges from $20,000 a year to $200,000. And a related career, professional horse riding, is covered through the profile in chapter 8.

The reason for omitting these sports careers from the scope of this book is that individuals tend to get into those careers through doing, not through reading. However, there are some work possibilities in sports for individuals who read. Anyone who has watched any televised sports, on the professional or collegiate level, may recall those persons on or behind the bench who carried clipboards or towels or dispensed drinks. Work in a position that supports professional athletes may not yield well-paying jobs and may, indeed, be purely volunteer. However, individuals who want to be near a sport (and outdoors at the same time) but cannot pursue it actively may gain great pleasure from this type of involvement.

SECOND CAREERS

Many people wishing to change jobs seriously consider outdoor work as part of a second (or even third or fourth) career. They have discovered, while working at other careers, that outdoor-type work is important for them. If this describes you, use the information you have learned about yourself on previous jobs as you read through this book to find an appropriate career in the outdoors.

Unfortunately, many outdoor jobs do not pay well; often, one of the major rewards of the career is simply being able to work in the outdoors. As the park ranger says in his profile: "We get paid in sunsets." Persons who have retired early from government or military service and have a full pension may be better able to take the lower salary than others who do not have the benefit of a second income.

WHERE TO GO FROM HERE

You may wish to obtain some of the materials listed in the Resources section at the end of each chapter. Another excellent way to get career information is to contact persons who are currently working in the field that interests you. A personal interview would be preferable, but depending on where you live, you may find it better to write. Because work settings play an important part in someone's reaction to a career, try to contact persons in several different types of settings. Prepare a list of questions about the career and ask for advice on getting into that field.

If you find it difficult to locate individuals, you may be able to obtain some member names from the appropriate organization or association, such as the American Society of Agricultural Engineers. A local high school or your alma mater may be able to give you names of graduates who have gone into a particular field, and a library may have information on companies with the types of jobs that interest you.

Individual accounts of a career must, however, be taken with a grain of salt. Every person has a unique work situation and a unique personality. If, for example, the first forester you contact is completely negative about the job, don't give up on this career area immediately. Try to find out why this person doesn't like the career, but also contact several others in different settings to get their perspectives. After all, the experts on any one career area are those who are currently engaged in that particular line of work.

WOMEN AND OUTDOOR CAREERS

Adequately covering the topic of women in outdoor careers is beyond the scope of this book, but it is a subject that cannot be ignored. While greater numbers of women are entering fields traditionally dominated by men and are represented in virtually every occupation described in this book, women continue to be underrepresented in most outdoor careers. Many factors contribute to this imbalance.

Although women in other cultures, like those in our pioneer past, perform many physically challenging tasks, most women today are not being culturally prepared or encouraged to consider outdoor work. Some outdoor careers, such as commercial diving, require a great deal of physical strength and an irregular lifestyle that make them unattractive to many women. Additionally, many women do not have the high school grounding in mathematics and science needed for certain technical fields such as engineering.

A lack of female role models or mentors has also contributed to the smaller number of women in outdoor careers. Women seeking to enter a male-dominated career may find it helpful to locate a woman mentor for encouragement. If no one is available in your area, professional societies may provide names and addresses of women in occupations that interest you.

Women now make up virtually half of the labor force. While women may never be fully represented in all areas of outdoor work, it is important that they, as well as men, be encouraged to explore fully the careers that interest them and for which they believe they are suited.

A FINAL WORD

Good luck as you explore your career options! Whether this is your first serious look for an appropriate career or you are considering a career change, the more knowledge you bring to your choice, the better your final decision will be.

RESOURCES

The following organizations have seasonal as well as full-time positions.

Appalachian Mountain Club
Five Joy Street
Boston, MA 02108
Telephone: 617-523-0636
Fax: 617-523-0722
Web: http://www.outdoors.org

National Outdoor Leadership School
288 Main Street
Lander, WY 82520
Telephone: 307-332-6973
Fax: 307-332-1220
Web: http://www.nols.edu

Outward Bound USA
Route 9D R–2 Box 280
Garrison, NY 10524
Telephone: 914-424-4000; 800-243-8520
Fax: 914-424-4280
Web: http://www.outwardbound.com

Student Conservation Association, Inc.
P.O. Box 550
Charlestown, NH 03603
Telephone: 603-543-1700
Fax: 603-543-1828
Web: http://www.sca-inc.org

For internship positions or volunteer work:

The Internship Bible. NY: Princeton Review, Random House, updated annually.

Volunteer America: A Comprehensive National Guide to Opportunities for Service, Training, and Work Experience, 4th ed. Chicago: Ferguson Publishing Company, 1997.

The Nature Conservancy
4245 North Fairfax Drive, Suite 100
Arlington, VA 22203-1606
Telephone: 703-841-5300
Fax: 703-841-1283
Web: http://www.tnc.org
Job Hotline: 703-247-3721

Chapter 1

Choosing Your Career

> *Successful careers seldom happen by chance. With very few*
> *exceptions people who really get what they want in a career do*
> *so because they define clear objectives, develop plans and*
> *schedules for achieving their objectives, assume personal*
> *responsibility for implementing and following these plans,*
> *monitor their progress regularly, improve their plans when*
> *they aren't getting the desired results, and persevere in the*
> *face of frequent setbacks until their objects are achieved.*
> Nicholas Weiler, *Reality and Career Planning*

People choose careers in various ways. Some simply accept any position that is available and looks interesting. Others take a job because they know someone who does that type of work or works for the same organization. Still others take time for some self-assessment to discover who they really are and what they can and want to do. They then research to learn what kinds of careers fit the type of person they are.

The fact that you have picked up this book probably means that you fall into this last category. Because many careers require extensive training, it is wise to research carefully before making your choice. Even if you are quite certain which career you wish to enter, take a little time to be sure you are headed in the best possible direction for the unique person you are.

One of the first steps in choosing a career is to complete a personal inventory. This will help you better define your unique characteristics and what you want to do. Important components are your interests, skills, and values.

You chose to read this book because the outdoors is important to you. What you need to decide is what role the outdoors should play in your career. Do you want to work outdoors, deal with a subject matter that relates to the outdoors, work for an organization that has outdoor concerns, or a combination of these? Consider these options as you continue to read this book.

INTERESTS

Your interests are one key factor in career decision making. It is important to select a field in which you will be working on issues, content, or subject matter that you care about. It is much more pleasant to spend thirty-five to forty hours a week doing work that greatly interests you than something that bores you. Being aware of your interests can help you identify potential work environments and employers.

As you work through the following exercises picking out your skills and values, use interest as a criterion to keep or eliminate items from your list. For example, although you may be skilled at drawing, you may not like to do it. Picking a career that uses a skill that doesn't interest you would be counterproductive—you would not really enjoy that career.

SKILLS

When you examine different careers, it's important to know whether your skills match those required for that career. If you have completed a skills inventory, you will be able to decide whether a particular career is a good fit for you.

A *skill* is generally defined as "something you do well." Some of your skills may come to mind immediately. But because we aren't always tuned in to the things we do well, it is a good idea to spend some time assessing your skills.

The list that follows contains some of the skills you should consider. As you read through these skills, write down those that apply to you. Consider skills you have used in clubs, extracurricular activities, or hobbies, as well as on jobs or in school.

administer	formulate	predict
analyze	fund-raise	print
arrange	guide	promote
assemble	interpret	question
build	interview	recruit
calculate	investigate	repair
coach	keep records	research
coordinate	listen	sell
counsel	manage	sketch
create	measure	speak publicly
delegate	mediate	supervise
design	negotiate	talk
dramatize	observe	teach
edit	organize	translate
evaluate	persuade	troubleshoot
explain	plan	write

This list is by no means exhaustive; you will want to add other skills that occur to you. Also, as you write down your skills, it's helpful to add an example of a situation when you used each one. For example, you might note under "keep records" that as a 4-H club treasurer for three years, you kept accurate records of the membership dues paid and the results of special sales projects.

VALUES

Also vital to consider when making a career choice are your values—those things that are most important to you. They provide satisfaction and add purpose and fulfillment to life. Often people do not realize that their values don't match those of their chosen profession until they are well into a career. Figuring out this part of the career match before you make other choices can help you avoid problems later on.

Read the following list and write down the values that are important to you.

achievement	perform important roles and be involved in momentous endeavors
autonomy	be free to work with little supervision and set your own schedule and priorities
distinction	be well known, be seen as successful, and have recognition and status in your chosen field
expertise	become a respected and trusted expert in your field
friendship	like and be liked by the people with whom you work
leadership	be an influential and respected leader
location	be able to live and work in the places you choose
pleasure	find enjoyment and have fun doing your work
power	be able to approve or disapprove different courses of action, make assignments, and control allocations and outcomes
security	obtain a secure and stable position
self-realization	do work that is challenging and allows you to fully develop your talents
service	help people in need and contribute to the satisfaction of others
wealth	earn a great deal of money so that you can be financially independent

Jot down any other values that are important to you. At this stage of the decision-making process, it is helpful to write down as much information about yourself as possible.

TEMPERAMENT AND PERSONAL QUALITIES

Take a few moments to examine your personality and temperament. Are you outgoing, patient, reflective, conscientious, or responsible? Which are your traits that you like best and would like to use on the job? Write these down.

SUMMER, PART-TIME, AND VOLUNTEER WORK

Knowing your interests, skills, values, and personal qualities will help you make a better match as you investigate the careers in this book. Another aid in deciding on a career is to actually do the type of work that interests you. Many outdoor jobs are available on a summer, part-time, or volunteer basis. A careful search can land you a summer or short-term job in the type of setting you believe best matches your needs and desires.

You may also want to check into volunteer work related to the field you're considering. Many communities have agencies that seek to match volunteers with jobs, and these can help you in your search. With a little persistence, however, you should be able to arrange your own volunteer position.

Working in the setting of a career that interests you—or at least in one that is similar—can help you decide whether you really want to get into that type of work. And the contacts you make in your summer, part-time, or volunteer work can be invaluable to you later when you actually begin your job search.

ADDITIONAL CAREER-SEARCH RESOURCES

At this point you may not yet be certain about the exact career that appeals to you and want to do some additional searching. Don't despair! Sometimes it simply takes a while to settle on a career. Doing some background research before you spend a lot of time and money preparing for a particular career is very worthwhile. Help is as close as your public library, bookstore, telephone, or Internet access point.

You may decide that you want a career counselor to help you identify your interests, skills, and values; locate resources to explore different career options; or prepare for the job search. A career counselor can help you by providing an objective eye; it is often difficult to see yourself clearly. Counselors are also helpful in guiding you through the self-evaluation process if you get stuck.

Career counselors can be located fairly easily. One place to look is at nearby colleges and universities, most of which offer career counseling to their students. Many extend free use of this service to their graduates, and some also serve the public, although usually for a fee. Nonprofit organizations, government agencies, and employment centers also offer career counseling, usually at little or no cost.

Private career counselors are usually quite good, although their fees will be higher, and many people find this type of counseling the most helpful. These counselors can be located in the yellow pages or through friends and relatives.

Before you invest too much time or money, make certain that the counselor will be helpful to you. Arrange for a fifteen-minute free visit to see whether you feel comfortable with him or her. A good personality match is important. Also find out whether the counselor is a Nationally Certified Career Counselor, shown by the acronym *NCCC* following his or her name. This certification indicates professional recognition, a commitment to continuing education, the passing of two national exams, recommendations from the field, and supervised experience.

You may choose to consult one of the excellent books that give in-depth assistance in making career decisions. The books recommended here should be available in libraries or bookstores. You may also locate books not on this list that are very helpful to you.

USING THE INTERNET

The Internet can also provide assistance in choosing your best career. Many career counseling services are available online. Again, though, take some care in selecting a service. The background, experience, and expertise of the counselor with whom you would be dealing are essential pieces of information. You should also determine the amount of assistance you can actually gain from a service. For example, does this service only help in self-assessment for choosing a career, or does it also provide help in the nitty-gritty of finding a job: preparing strategies for the job search, writing a résumé, locating job possibilities, and preparing for an interview? You will also want to evaluate carefully the charges for the service to determine whether you will be getting your money's worth.

For more information about using the Internet in your job search, see chapter 10. Be sure to check the Resources listing at the end of that chapter.

RESOURCES

Bolles, Richard Nelson. *What Color Is Your Parachute? A Practical Manual for Job-Hunters & Career Changers.* Berkeley, Calif.: Ten Speed Press, updated annually.

Dyer, Paul L. *The Ultimate Job Search Survival Guide.* Princeton, N.J.: Peterson's Guides, 1998.

Farr, Mike. *The Very Quick Job Search,* 2d ed. Indianapolis: JIST Works, 1996.

Gilman, Cheryl. *Doing Work You Love.* Lincolnwood, Ill.: Contemporary Books, 1997.

Kennedy, Joyce Lain, and Darryl Laramore. *Joyce Lain Kennedy's Career Book,* 3d ed. Lincolnwood, Ill.: VGM, 1997.

———. *Hook Up, Get Hired! The Internet Job Search Revolution.* New York: Wiley, 1995.

Kipps, Harriet Clyde, ed. *Volunteer America: A Comprehensive National Guide to Opportunities for Service, Training, and Work Experience,* 4th ed. Chicago: Ferguson Publishing Company, 1997.

Krannich, Ronald L., and Caryl Krannich. *Discover the Best Jobs for You,* 3d ed. Manassas, Va.: Impact Publications, 1998.

———. *Change Your Job: Change Your Life.* Manassas, Va.: Impact Publications, 1997.

Lorenzen, Elizabeth A., ed. *Career Planning and Job Searching in the Information Age.* Binghamton, N.Y.: Haworth Press, 1996.

Maestas, Lily, and Lorelei Snyder. *Unlimited Options: Career Strategies to Last a Lifetime.* Santa Barbara, Calif.: Prosperity Press, 1996.

A few helpful Web sites:

What Color Is My Parachute, electronic edition (http://www.washingtonpost.com/wp=adv/classi).

The Career Interests Game (http://www.missouri.edu/~cppcww/holland.html) from the University of Missouri is based on the Holland system, which classifies personality types and work environments into six groups: realistic, investigative, artistic, social, enterprising, and conventional.

The site from the University of North Texas (http://www.unt.edu/coc/) has links to sixteen career sites: click on Career Search and the Internet Guide, then click on Personal Assessment. Or after you have clicked on Career Search and the Internet Guide, scroll to the bottom and select either Best of the Career Search Sites or Mega Career Search Web Sites.

At http://campus.monster.com/ you can get a great variety of career information by selecting different options from the opening page.

Chapter 2

Agriculture and Food Production

There's no beginning to the farmer's year
Only recurrent patterns on a scroll
Unwinding.

Vita Sackville-West, "Spring," *The Land*

Farming, one of the oldest of outdoor occupations, is an appropriate place to begin looking at outdoor careers. When North America was settled by European immigrants, the small farm was one means of "taming" the wilderness. The land was cleared, plowed, planted, and harvested. As the country grew, the U.S. government encouraged this development through land grant policies, homesteading acts, and the sale of land at low cost. As a result, the U.S. farm economy is based on the family farm unit: The farmer owns or rents land and manages the total resource.

With the advent of machinery to aid in harvesting, such as the cotton gin and the harvester, many farms in the nineteenth century grew beyond the scope of the small family operation into plantations or large farms specializing in one crop, such as cotton, tobacco, wheat, or sugar beets. The trend has been toward a decrease in the total percentage of the labor force employed in farming. The number of individual farm operations has declined, as farms have been combined by either purchase or lease. Despite this trend toward larger and larger farms, smaller farms can still be successfully and profitably operated.

This chapter examines careers related to the various types of farming, agriculture, and food production. It also suggests alternate methods of organizing a farming operation through profiles of people who have successfully bucked the agricultural trend toward large enterprises.

AGRONOMY

Salary Range	Starting between $21,500 and $26,500; with master's degrees, between $25,500 and $32,500; with Ph.D., $35,500 and up
Educational Requirements	College
Employment Outlook	Good

Agronomy is the scientific examination of crop production through the study of plants, soils, and the surrounding environment. The two main fields within agronomy are crop science and soil science.

Crop science looks at production of quality seeds that will yield larger crops and crops of higher nutritional value. Crop scientists examine all of the problems—including weeds, diseases, and insects—that inhibit crop development. In the process they study details such as genetics, cellular biology and molecular genetics, breeding, physiology, and managing field and turf crops. Crops that are considered include alfalfa, corn, cotton, sugarcane, peanuts, rice, soybeans, sunflowers, turf grass, and wheat.

Soil science examines the soils in their natural environment and as they relate to growing plants. The physics, chemistry, origin, microbiology, mineralogy, fertility, and management of the soil are all probed. The soils are characterized and the best uses for each type of soil determined. Soil scientists study other aspects of soil uses as well, such as reclamation, waste disposal, building foundations and road construction, and waterways.

A challenging field, agronomy offers an opportunity to use science to help increase the supply of high-quality crops while working to protect and preserve the environment. Agriculture in North America is very productive, and there are currently no great concerns about the quantity or quality of food. The challenge to agronomists, however, is to meet food-shortage problems around the world by helping areas with limited food production resources to use their resources more efficiently.

Agronomic research is highly technical, requiring very specific training and the use of some research tools such as computers, scanning electron microscopes, radioisotope detectors, satellites, and telemetry units. Use of these tools involves a creative imagination and acute observational skills. Knowledge of both physical sciences (chemistry, physics, and mathematics) and natural sciences (biology and geology) may be required to solve the problems agronomists tackle. Other scientists with whom agronomists may work closely include biochemists, microbiologists, entomologists, geneticists, plant pathologists, and agricultural economists and engineers.

Genetic engineering is an expanding field within agronomy that seeks to improve plants by transferring desirable genes, using discoveries made in genetics, molecular biology, physiology, biochemistry, and tissue and cell culture. Plants that are more insect or disease resistant may be developed, or their amino acid content may be improved to make the product more nutritious. This is a team-oriented field that offers great challenges. At the end of the twentieth century genetic engineering is seeing quite a lot of growth, and much attention is being given to new genetically engineered crops under development and the issues they raise.

The necessary course background for agronomists focuses on the sciences, including biology, chemistry, mathematics, physics, geology, botany, and microbiology. Applied science courses in areas such as genetics, plant pathology, soil chemistry, plant physiology, and biochemistry will also assist in preparation for an agronomy career. Knowledge of languages other than English is helpful for work within the United States and abroad.

Agronomists work in varied settings. Some are educators who teach and work with college students, informing them and seeking to interest them in further studies in agronomy. Extension agronomists also work with people; farmers and other groups who face problems often contact agricultural extension services, which are located at land grant colleges. Agronomists may also serve an educational and service function in industry by sharing their detailed knowledge about a company's services or products.

The soil conservation and forest services provide government employment for many agronomists. Urban projects such as zoning, parklands, land-use planning, and highway landscaping increasingly involve agronomists. Overseas agronomic job opportunities are available through government programs, aid groups, and philanthropic foundations, as well as large agricultural industries.

Other types of work in agronomy include research in industry, sales of agricultural products, and professional consulting services. Many people who have studied agronomy become farmers or ranchers and use their training to produce food or fiber crops. Agronomists also work as farm managers, bank loan specialists, and superintendents of golf courses or forests, as well as in top administrative positions in industry.

BEEKEEPING (APICULTURE)

Salary Range	Varies tremendously
Educational Requirements	Self-study or on-the-job training
Employment Outlook	Fair

Close to a third of the food eaten in North America comes either directly or indirectly from plants that have been pollinated by insects. Crops that rely on honeybees for this pollination include almonds, cucumbers, apples, avocados, blueberries, cantaloupes, cherries, pears, and watermelons. In the process of gathering the nectar needed for honey production, bees also pick up pollen from the different plants. As bees gather nectar from different plants, the pollen is transferred from plant to plant, fertilizing the plants. This fertilization allows the plants to reproduce.

Apiculturists focus on bee research. They may research bee diseases and how to control them. They may also experiment with breeding to produce hardier and more disease-resistant bees. Another area of study is the effects of pollination on bees.

Beekeepers' work involves gathering honey and placing bees where their pollination will directly benefit farmers. A beekeeper will make certain that a hive is in good repair, the colony and queen bee are healthy and flourishing, and the bees have enough food to maintain themselves. A great deal of the work is done outdoors, except for some maintenance tasks and record keeping.

Experience, gained from working with a beekeeper or by investing in a few hives, is all you need to get into this career. If you're interested in commercial beekeeping you'll want to consider some schooling, though—either a two- or a four-year program with some apiculture courses.

Beekeepers are mainly hobbyists or part-time workers; only a small number do commercial work. Some raise bees to sell, and as the number of bee hobbyists increases, this option may offer more possibilities.

Those with a bachelor's degree and experience may find work as state inspectors. A doctorate is needed to qualify for research with the U.S. Department of Agriculture or a university. Some areas of research include problems facing bees, the nectar and pollen yields of plants, and the content of honey. College teaching and working for a commercial bee firm are other options for apiculturists.

FARM MANAGEMENT

Salary Range	From $16,500 to $65,000, depending on the size and number of operations managed
Educational Requirements	College plus continuing education
Employment Outlook	Declining, and competition for positions is keen

A farm manager operates farms owned by others. Farm managers have a wide range of duties; they may be assigned to one activity, such as feeding livestock, or to the entire operation of a farm. In fact, one manager may be in charge of as many as thirty-five farm units at one time. This position requires knowledge of both agricultural practices and business methods. Exact duties vary according to the size and type of farm managed and the amount of authority delegated by the owner.

A manager's duties involve organizing and administering farm work; determining labor needs; and hiring, supervising, and, when necessary, firing employees. The farm manager organizes schedules for planting, harvesting, and marketing. He or she determines land use and the best agricultural methods. Other functions may include the purchase of supplies and equipment, the maintenance and upkeep of equipment and buildings, the care and feeding of livestock, and some marketing and accounting.

For the farm manager, work involves a great deal of walking and many outdoor duties. At times the job may involve operating farm equipment. Traveling between farms managed and to the office is also necessary. Hours at work vary according to the season; during busy periods the manager often works more than an eight-hour day.

A farm manager should be able to work well with other individuals, because he or she must answer to the owner and also supervise workers. Other requirements are the ability to objectively evaluate new developments, techniques, and machinery, and to do detailed planning.

Good background for farm management is involvement in a 4-H club or the Future Farmers of America to gain both training and experience. A bachelor of science degree in an area related to agriculture is helpful; courses should include agricultural economics, business, agronomy, and animal science. Continuing professional education will help the manager keep informed of new methods and procedures.

Opportunities in this field are limited because of an overall decline in the industry. Competition for available jobs is intense, and the edge will go to individuals with specialized training and extensive experience or agricultural background. Professional farm managers may be hired by a commercial bank or an independent farm management firm, or they may be self-employed.

FARMING

Salary Range	Varies tremendously, depending on type of farm and weather conditions each year, but an estimate is $16,500 to $68,000
Educational Requirements	None, although college is a distinct asset
Employment Outlook	Poor

You'll find a great variety of farm types, generally categorized by farm product. In almost none of them is growth expected, largely because of the current trend toward consolidating farmlands into larger-sized farms. With the exception of dairy, livestock, and poultry farms—which are run year-round—much of the work is highly seasonal. Farmers often work elsewhere during the off season to supplement their farm income. Following are basic descriptions of the types of farming. Dairy farming, though not a growth area, may be easier to get into than the others.

Cotton, Tobacco, and Peanut
Cotton, tobacco, and peanuts are among the major crops grown, although tobacco growing has begun to decline. Usually a farmer grows only one of these crops, because each requires a very different farming method.

Grain
Grains grown include corn, wheat, rye, and grain sorghums, which are used as food for both people and animals. Although grain production is increasing, this is mainly because of improved farming methods that enable bigger crops to be raised on fewer acres.

Dairy
The major dairy-farming products are cows, which are bred and raised, and milk, which is supplied to the milk and milk-products industries. Unlike most types of farms, these provide a year-round income. Many dairy farmers also grow crops as feed for their herds and have a self-sustaining operation.

Livestock

The major types of livestock raised for profit—cattle, hogs, sheep, and goats—are raised for food or for their hides or hair. Other livestock farmers raise horses, mules, or donkeys as draft animals to pull heavy loads. Large horse farms also focus on horses for racing or pleasure. Some farmers raise only one type of animal, but others raise a number of different types and also grow the crops to feed them.

Poultry

Chickens, turkeys, and ducks are raised on poultry farms, which usually specialize in one type of production, such as meat, eggs, or breeding.

Fruit

Fruits grown and marketed for profit include citrus varieties, apples, pears, peaches, berries, melons, nuts, and grapes.

Vegetable

Some of the vegetables raised for profit are beans, potatoes, corn, carrots, tomatoes, lettuce, and peppers. Soybeans are valuable both as food and for their many products, such as oil and soy sauce. Their high nutritional content makes them an important product. The size of vegetable farms and the methods of marketing range from small farms with roadside stands to farms larger than 150 acres that employ field hands.

See Profiles, pages 19 and 21.

HERB GROWING AND MARKETING

Salary Range	Varies tremendously
Educational Requirements	None, although college is an asset
Employment Outlook	Uncertain; this is a developing field

Herb growing and marketing is a fairly new field that is becoming more important as herb use increases. Herb businesses are usually small or medium-sized home-based operations, often involving only the owner or fewer than five employees.

Many people begin growing herbs as a hobby and find that it gradually evolves into more. Very little education is available specifically for growing herbs, but a solid background in farming is helpful. Some universities do have departments that emphasize herb production. Because a wide variety of species are involved in herb growing, some knowledge of taxonomy—the classification of plants in relation to other plants—is becoming more important. For individuals in their own business, knowledge of marketing is helpful, because commercial herb production is still somewhat new and the markets are not readily defined.

Individuals in the United States who wish to work for an herb company will probably need to relocate, because the larger companies seem to be concentrated in certain parts of the country. Generally, there aren't many jobs advertised in this field; you'll need to make direct contacts with businesses for which you wish to work.

Those interested in pursuing this career should contact some of the existing organizations or networks. These offer valuable contacts and information from newsletters and association meetings.

RANGE MANAGEMENT

Salary Range	Starting at about $17,200 and topping off at about $35,000
Educational Requirements	College
Employment Outlook	Growing, although somewhat dependent on federal funding

Rangelands constitute about 45 percent of the world's land—they're the world's most plentiful type of land. This broad category includes natural grasslands, shrub communities, forests, savannas, tundra, wetlands, alpine communities, and most deserts. Native to these lands are grasses, shrubs, and broad-leafed plants. The basic means of food production from rangelands is through livestock grazing.

Range management has become a specific discipline only in the last fifty years. It takes into account ecology and ways to manage the range ecosystems to yield desired products in a natural and economical manner. Rangeland specialists deal with everything that affects the range: soil, water, plants, animals, and climate. Much of the work throughout the year will be done out on the range in all types of weather, but range specialists also spend time in the office keeping records. Some may be college teachers and may also spend time in research.

Required education is a bachelor of science degree in a major such as range science, range management, or range ecology. Basic required courses are botany, biology, chemistry, math, statistics, English, and public speaking. Specialized courses are genetics, ecology, climate, biochemistry, soil science, animal science and nutrition, plant taxonomy, physiology, and geology.

Public relations skills are important for range managers. They must work with people and earn their trust, whether they are handing down government rulings or dealing with ranchers, oil workers, hunters and fishers, or government workers. They may also need to work in cooperation with specialists in areas such as wildlife, hydrology, forestry, soils, and recreation.

Most jobs for rangeland specialists are in different federal government departments. Some jobs also exist in state and local governments. Increasingly, jobs are becoming available in private industry. These include ranch managers; research, sales, and service representatives for commercial companies; and bank consultants or advisers. Range management is a good major for people who plan to become ranchers. The number of jobs in this area is likely to remain constant; positions will open up mainly through attrition.

The agency or institution job titles for individuals who are trained range scientists vary widely. Because the interest in all aspects of the environment continues to grow, the projection is for a 33 percent increase in positions for range scientists over the next decade. This projection is above the normal attrition that occurs every year.

RURAL APPRAISAL

Salary Range	Starting at about $20,000, averaging about $45,000, and topping off at about $65,000
Educational Requirements	College plus license and continuing education
Employment Outlook	Good in states with rural properties; competition for positions is keen

A rural appraiser estimates the value of rural real estate. Appraisers decide the market value of a property so that taxes; a selling price; rental payments; the legal distribution of property among people; or the assets of individuals, firms, or corporations can be determined.

The appraiser must collect and interpret data on the property, such as the condition and maintenance; the type of rent or ownership; and the cost of real estate taxes, insurance, maintenance, services, and other expenses.

Appraisers must travel to property sites to inspect and examine them. This involves work outdoors, measuring and walking throughout each property to evaluate it. A major part of the work is done in the office, however, studying collected data, writing reports, and maintaining records.

Rural appraisers need to learn about land values and economic conditions and should have an agricultural degree with courses in real estate, business, economics, and journalism. Because some governments require licensing, continuing education is necessary. Important personal characteristics include honesty, integrity, and tact, as well as accuracy, attention to detail, good oral and written communication skills, and the ability to interpret data.

Earnings of rural appraisers vary considerably, depending especially on experience, training, and the geographic location. Some rural appraisers are employed by federal and state agencies and by insurance companies; others are self-employed. Hours may be irregular, ranging from fewer than twenty-five to more than fifty hours a week.

The demand for rural appraisers is higher in areas such as the western United States, where there is a large amount of rural property. The number of jobs is expected to remain constant; workers will be needed to replace those who retire or leave the career. Competition for available positions is expected to be keen, and the edge will go to well-trained and experienced individuals.

RESOURCES

Agronomy, Crops, and Soils

American Society of Agronomy/Crop Science
Society of America/Soil Science Society of America
677 South Segoe Road
Madison, WI 53711
Telephone: 608-273-8080
Fax: 608-273-2021
Web: http://www.agronomy.org

Beekeeping

The American Beekeeping Federation, Inc.
P.O. Box 1038
Jessup, GA 31598-1038
Telephone: 912-427-4233
Fax: 912-427-8447
Web: http://www.abfnet.org

Farm Management and Rural Appraisal

American Society of Farm Managers and Rural Appraisers
950 South Cherry Street, Suite 508
Denver, CO 80222
Telephone: 303-758-3513
Fax: 303-758-0190
Web: http://www.agri-associations.org

Agriculture

American Horticultural Society
7931 East Boulevard Drive
Alexandria, VA 22308
Telephone: 703-768-5700
Web: http://www.ahs.org/

National Agriculture Library
Agricultural Research Service
U.S. Department of Agriculture
10305 Baltimore Avenue
Beltsville, MD 20705
Telephone: 301-504-5755
Web: http://www.usda.gov

Agriculture and Agri-Food Canada
Sir John Carling Building
930 Carling Avenue
Ottawa, Ontario K1A 0C7
Telephone: 613-759-1000
Fax: 613-759-7977
Web: http://www.aceis.agr.ca/newintre.htm

Economic Research Division
American Farm Bureau Federation
225 Touhy Avenue
Park Ridge, IL 60068
Telephone: 312-399-5700
Fax: 312-399-5896
Web: http://www.fb.com

The Canadian Federation of Agriculture
75 Albert Street, Suite 1101
Ottawa, Ontario K1P 5E7
Telephone: 613-236-3633
Web: http://www.cfa-fca.ca/careers/indextop.html

Organic Farming and Community-Supported Agriculture

Sylvia and Walter Ehrhardt
1032 Hoffmaster Road
Knoxville, MD 21758
Telephone: 301-834-9247
Fax: 310-834-5070
Web: http://www.digmazine.com/writers/sylvia

Organic Farming Research Foundation
P.O. Box 440
Santa Cruz, CA 95061
Telephone: 831-426-6606
Fax: 831-426-6670
Web: http://www.ofrf.org

Herb Growing

International Herb Growers & Marketers Network
P.O. Box 245
Silver Spring, PA 17575-0245
Telephone: 717-393-3295
Fax: 717-393-9261
Web: http://www.herbworld.com or http://www.herb-net.com

Ontario Herbalists Association
11 Winthrop Place
Stoney Creek, Ontario L8G 3M3
Telephone and fax: 416-536-1509
Web: http://www.herbalists.on.ca/

Range Management

> Society for Range Management
> 1839 York Street
> Denver, CO 80206
> Telephone: 303-355-7070
> Fax: 303-355-5059
> Web: http://www.srm.org

Profile

DAIRY FARMER
Valentine Yutzy

"You don't have to get big to get good," dairy farmer Valentine Yutzy says emphatically. "In my opinion, no farm or factory should be allowed to operate until it reduces waste to the lowest common denominator."

Yutzy is out of sync with conventional ideas about farming in the midwestern United States. A farmer since 1963, Yutzy and his wife, Anne, have farmed the 240-acre Kramer Homestead in Plain City, Ohio, since 1972. Three families are currently supported by the farm, which according to conventional wisdom is too small to maintain this many people. In fact, the farm has been so profitable that the families annually divide between $18,000 and $20,000 in bonuses and also defer income to reduce taxes.

Yutzy, who was recently named Ohio State Conservationist of the Year and listed as one of the top ten conservationists in the nation, practices what is known in agronomy as a closed system. Yutzy explains what this means: "We try to raise all the feed needed for our livestock, and we also try to feed all the grain and forage that we raise. We then use our waste products [manure and crop residue] as our primary nutrients for future crops. In other words, we try to balance our agronomy and animal husbandry enterprises and do most of our marketing in milk and meat. We try to get these two enterprises to complement each other so that we need to buy very few outside inputs for our farming operation. We process our own soybeans for protein and energy [fat] supplementation of feed rations."

Yutzy practices conservation in four major areas: water-quality enhancement (by preventing nonfiltered surface runoff into streams); improvement of soil life and tilth (the part of the surface soil affected by tillage); prevention of soil erosion; and energy conservation. "One of the things we have been able to achieve," Yutzy reports, "is that our amount of electrical use in 1989 was almost identical to that of 1969, yet our farm has had normal expansion."

Although he hadn't finished high school, Yutzy spent two years in college as a premed student in the early 1960s. He was accepted by the medical school of Ohio State University, but with three young children, he chose instead to go into farming in 1963. Yutzy says that the science courses he took during those two years provided him with a foundation in the natural sciences.

He has since studied agronomy, but Yutzy does not call himself an agronomist. "A farmer needs to be a jack-of-many-trades and also a master of as many as possible," Yutzy says. "Or, in other words, I need to be a generalist to see all the parts of the whole and also a specialist to be able to expertly function in one part." Yutzy is also self-trained in ecology, engineering ("building design, heating and ventilation, and electrical and mechanical applications"), marketing, and animal husbandry.

Yutzy farms in partnership with his two sons, and the three families hire very little outside help. They do most of their own building and repair work, as well as necessary mechanical and electrical work.

Personable and an easy conversationalist, Yutzy is adamant that size does not determine quality. "Free-enterprise business courses generally teach that if you are not growing, then you are going backward. On the contrary, I think that quality must always supersede quantity." He adds, "We here in America have moved toward bigness as a sign of individual success, to the long-term detriment of ecology and opportunity."

Yutzy's farming philosophy builds on his own personal philosophy. "I believe that we are stewards of what God has given us," he says with quiet conviction. "If we become possessors of it, we handle things in a much different way than if we are stewards of it, handling it for somebody else. When we are possessors of it, we can be too willing to take a risk, we think too highly of our own abilities, and we want to make a quick dollar. What we really need to do is to handle it and pass it on to the next generation in as good or better shape than it was when we got it."

Yutzy has this advice for those who want to get into dairy farming: "If you want to have fifty cows, get twenty-five heifer calves in April and start feeding them. That's not a big expense. Get another twenty-five two months later, and do the same the next year. You will cull better than 50 percent, but you won't have nearly the expense if you raise them yourself as if you buy them all ready to milk. You will also learn if you can raise your own replacements, which you need to do to have a successful dairy.

So start out by being sure that you can raise your own replacements. When they are two years old, start milking in a stanchion barn where you walk in among the animals. That way you learn to know the animals and how to be responsive to their needs. Then you can move into a parlor where you aren't closely associated with the animals, if that's what you want to do.

"One of my philosophies," Yutzy relates with a chuckle, "is that you make more money thinking than you do working." As the senior farm operator, he usually spends several hours on the telephone each morning doing business and planning the general running of the farm. "My time outside varies," he says. "Sometimes I spend all day outside doing physical work and sometimes I'm out very little." A computer is very useful in farm operation. It provides accessible information and has a program to formulate the mix of corn, soybeans, and other ingredients for the animals' feed. The computer doesn't necessarily save time, however; Yutzy spends at least an hour a day keeping it up to date.

Yutzy is optimistic about the future of farming. "No matter what else happens in the world, people will still have to have food. I think we need a different emphasis in what we produce so that we produce quality first and then quantity." In fact, he predicts that this is the future for agriculture: "In the future, quality is going to be much more in demand. I don't see anything but a good future for the farmer who is capable of working with the laws of nature and the biological aspect of farming."

See Farming, page 12.

Profile

ORGANIC FARMERS
Sylvia and Walter Ehrhardt

For organic farmers Sylvia and Walter Ehrhardt, it all began when they read the book *Living the Good Life* by Helen and Scott Nearing. The Nearings wrote about their move to the country after they realized that they wanted more from life than working in the city. "When I read of the pleasure they experienced living near the earth, watching the seasons change, and growing their own vegetables, something resonated very deep within me," Sylvia relates.

At that time, in 1972, the Ehrhardts lived and worked in Washington, D.C. Deciding to change their lives, they began taking agriculture courses and exploring their options. In late 1979 Sylvia left her public relations job in the Carter White House, and they moved to Knoxville, Maryland, just across the Potomac from Harpers Ferry, West Virginia.

Their whole seventy-six-acre tract was in trees, so their initial challenge was to clear land. Then they planted strawberries, blackberries, red raspberries, and miniature squash. By 1981 they were supplying restaurants as far away as Washington, D.C. Walter initially kept his position in the Department of Housing and Urban Development on a part-time basis but quit altogether in 1986.

"We wanted to create our own environment," says Sylvia of their move. "When we cleared land to build our home, we took out only the trees we wanted out." Over the years they have continued to clear land at the rate of a half acre a year.

They also began to change the emphasis of their farm. In 1987 they spoke to a group of chemically sensitive people, who asked if the Ehrhardts could provide them with organically grown vegetables. All of the agriculture courses Sylvia was taking were chemically oriented, and when she inquired she was told it was not possible to farm organically. So they began to attend conferences and workshops and joined an organic growers' association. "We did lots of research and reading," she explains, "and then we learned through trial and error."

By 1990 they'd begun a pick-your-own operation—people came to the farm to pick berries—although they still supplied a few local restaurants. They then changed the major focus of the farm to community-supported agriculture, a Japanese style of farming that brings consumers and growers together.

Sylvia explains: "People buy shares, at $360 for a full share for twenty weeks. In return, we provide enough in-season vegetables, herbs, and berries to serve two to four persons weekly. We pack quantities in one- to two-quart containers and put everything into shopping bags, and people come by once a week to pick up their food." The Ehrhardts now support the equivalent of fifty-three families (some have bought half shares).

The Ehrhardts' daughter manages the farm, and both Sylvia and Walter work there. Additionally, they usually have two interns, who work four hours a day in exchange for room and board and information about organic farming. Occasionally the Ehrhardts also hire neighbors to help with the harvest.

As their knowledge and practice of organic farming have grown, their work has changed, Sylvia says. "We now give workshops and have groups coming to look at our operation. We're starting to use the farm as an organic-farming demonstration and training center."

Sylvia is enthusiastic about community-supported agriculture. "It is one of the most exciting concepts I've come across. It cuts out the middleman and does not cost as much as a co-op. It provides an equitable amount for everyone. We figured out last year that each person who paid $360 received $600 worth of food.

"The small farmer needs to know about this concept," she continues. "You do not have to be big and own heavy equipment to succeed in farming. One acre, if planted intensively, can grow enough food for twenty-five people. And farmers certainly do not have to farm organically in order to operate this way."

The Ehrhardts have found that other countries are also interested in this concept. In fact, they took a trip to eastern Europe in the fall of 1991 to talk about their experiences. "We have a small acreage and we are living from this," explains Sylvia. "A lot of people want to know about it."

The major bonus for the Ehrhardts is the lifestyle, but they are making a profit as well. "If we wanted to make lots of money, we would expand the acre we are farming," Sylvia explains. "As it is, we have our own honey—we have six hives—and our own food to freeze and process."

She says that she is very happy they made this change in lifestyle. "I only wish I had done it earlier. Living near nature this way is much more sane. I like the city and many things about the city. Now we can combine the best of the city and the country so that we really do have a good life."

See Farming, page 12.

Chapter 3

Biological Sciences

*There is one quality that characterizes all of us who deal with
the sciences of the earth and its life—we are never bored.*
                                                    Rachel Carson

Because biology is the study of living things and their life processes, it is commonly known as the life sciences. Life scientists are interested in the beginnings and the protection of all forms of life, from the tiniest cell to the largest animal.

The life sciences may be approached as either basic or applied sciences. Those who work in basic biology are mainly interested in the study of living things. In contrast, applied biologists look for knowledge that will improve the world; for example, they may work in agriculture to improve crop production.

The field of biology contains many broad disciplines, with opportunities for specialization in each one. They include aquatic biology, the study of plants and animals that live in fresh water; botany, the study of plants; ecology, the study of the relationship of organisms to the environment; mycology, the study of fungi; taxonomy, the study of genetic relationships among species; and zoology, or animal biology, the study of animals. The related field of veterinary medicine is also covered in this chapter.

Biologists work in widely varied settings. By far the largest number work in institutions of higher learning. They are not all teachers, however; research and laboratory positions are also available at universities and colleges. Many biologists work for private business or industry in positions involving research, testing, product improvement, and sales. Biologists at colleges and universities may also be employed by industries as special consultants.

One industry in which biologists can find research positions is the pharmaceutical industry; in fact, research is its foundation. Even as these companies were looking to cut costs in the 1990s, their demand for research positions remained relatively stable.

Governments at all levels—federal, state, and municipal—employ almost a quarter of all biology graduates. These job settings include national parks and monuments, agricultural research stations, and museums. A smaller percentage of biologists work for nonprofit organizations.

AQUATIC BIOLOGY

Salary Range	Varies widely, depending on education, experience, location, and type of job; beginning at about $17,000, averaging $37,500, and topping off at about $68,000
Educational Requirements	College degree at the minimum
Employment Outlook	Good

An aquatic biologist studies the plants and animals that live in a freshwater ecosystem. (A marine biologist is the saltwater equivalent.) The basic academic background necessary for an aquatic biologist is a bachelor's degree in biological sciences. The course load should emphasize the natural sciences and should also be strong in the physical sciences.

A bachelor's degree qualifies you for an introductory job, while some additional experience or a master's degree is necessary for an intermediate job. Advanced jobs will go to candidates with doctorates or substantial experience.

Positions in aquatic biology are often among the first to be cut when governments face a financial squeeze. Since environmental problems are of great concern, private companies have expanded to fill many gaps left by government cutbacks; specialization in the field will open additional positions. Two areas of specialization are effluent toxicity testing, dealing with the wastes that are discharged into the environment, and hydraulics, which involves determining the amount of water needed in a fish habitat and timing the amount released from a dam.

See Profile, page 42.

BOTANY

Salary Range	Depends on education, experience, location, and type of job; beginning at about $24,000, with $35,000 as a median income, and about $43,000 as the maximum
Educational Requirements	At least a bachelor's degree
Employment Outlook	Good, especially for those with a doctorate, because of environmental and food-supply concerns

Botany (or plant science) is the study of plants, from tiny organisms to giant trees. The variety of fields within botany is enormous, and the work settings are diverse. Botanists include many kinds of plant biologists and some interrelated specialists. The varied career opportunities within the field are an attractive feature of the plant sciences.

Work settings include universities and research institutes. The U.S. Agricultural Research Service (ARS), part of the Department of Agriculture, is one government department that hires plant scientists. Headquartered in Beltsville, Maryland, the ARS conducts research across the United States.

Botany careers that have the greatest potential for outdoor work are plant taxonomy, plant exploration, plant pathology, and plant physiology. Botanists may also find outdoor work opportunities as resource managers in state heritage programs or by doing fieldwork.

Two areas of botany that have become separate disciplines—agronomy and forestry—are covered in chapters 2 and 4, respectively.

Plant Taxonomy

Plant taxonomists identify and classify different plants. In their work they spend part of their time outdoors gathering information and part indoors examining the data gathered. Tropical rain forests, which contain many plant species not yet cataloged, are one location where plant taxonomists may work to find new species. During the 1990s the U.S. government's emphasis on wetlands preservation opened up other areas in which to work. Whether more opportunities develop is largely dependent on government policy; in the United States the policies of the administration elected in 2000 will have a great effect on growth in this area. Plant taxonomy remains, however, a narrow specialty, and if the field does not expand it will, at least, complement other work in botany.

An example of work that a plant taxonomist can do in the field is consulting in wetlands evaluation when required by current laws. A consultant would be called by real estate agents and the local planning commission to determine whether areas where people wish to build homes are viable wetlands. Another job for a taxonomist is identifying endangered plant species, and plant taxonomists often travel to do this research. They collect plants in mild weather, and in the winter research in their laboratories.

A variety of employers hire plant taxonomists, although these jobs are often advertised as *ecologists* or *environmentalists* instead of *plant taxonomists*. One employer is the U.S. Army, which has hired people to identify vegetation and learn how much damage has been caused by war games in different locations throughout the country. Botanical gardens and institutions, such as the Smithsonian Institution in Washington, D.C., also have some positions for taxonomists. One unusual position with a Texas oil company involved in exploration used the taxonomist's skill in identifying pollen grains. The type of pollen present helped indicate whether they were close to oil.

Plant taxonomy is a narrow specialization in the field of botany. If current environmental concerns, such as wetlands preservation, remain high there could be more opportunities in this field. It is difficult to predict how this will develop.

Plant Exploration

Plant explorers are involved in searching out species of plants that are not yet classified—which may be interesting as species, but may also be very important for what they might contribute to life on our planet. A new food crop or drugs that can be used to cure or treat diseases may be discovered. Plants that are not yet classified might also be used to aid in genetic engineering by contributing to the plant gene pool.

This is a field with potential that has yet to be fully tapped. In fact, many of the available positions are not actually titled *plant explorer*; the job titles include *field researcher, international sourcing specialist, plant collector,* and *research ethnobotanist*. People in these positions do not necessarily go into the jungle searching for plants; they may talk with native people in their search.

Ethnobotany, a subfield within the area of plant exploration, studies the medicinal and other uses of plants by particular groups of people, such as Native Americans. Ethnobotany was the focus of the 1992 film, *Medicine Man*.

Most plant exploration positions are with research or academic institutions. Private agribusiness employers, such as Monsanto and Native Plants, Inc., have some positions, as do cosmetics and pharmaceutical companies; they are not major employers, however. Pharmaceutical companies often contract these positions out to workers in the country where the exploration is taking place. This is a career with as yet unrealized potential.

Plant Pathology

Plant pathologists are scientists who specialize in keeping plants healthy. They must know about the organisms that cause diseases in plants and affect the growth, yield, or quality of the plant product, understand how plants grow and how they're affected by disease, and know the basics of several disciplines related to plant pathology, including biochemistry, botany, ecology, epidemiology, genetics, microbiology, molecular biology, and physiology.

Plant diseases are caused by a variety of living organisms and by nonliving factors such as pollutants in the air and imbalances in nutrition. The living organisms, or pathogens, include protozoans, fungi, parasitic plants, nematodes, bacteria, and viruses. Plant pathologists are constantly challenged to deal with new diseases and changes in organisms that threaten our food crops, plants, and forests.

Plant pathologists may select from several approaches to manage plant diseases. One approach is to change the environmental conditions that cause the disease. Another is to change the host plant; one method of doing this is to develop resistant varieties of plants. A third approach is to alter the pathogen causing the disease by, for example, using a substance that destroys the pathogen but does not harm the environment or the plant.

Plant pathologists work both in laboratories and in the field examining crops or diseased plants. They identify diseases and experiment with various methods of treatment to find a cure for the diseases. Sophisticated laboratory research usually involves the use of an electron microscope and computer technology. Cooperation with specialists in other disciplines, such as organic chemistry, is important to discover and develop new means of controlling plant diseases.

Most plant pathologists major in one of the biological sciences for undergraduate study and then study plant pathology at the graduate level. Some jobs are available for those with a bachelor's degree in areas such as managing farms and greenhouses, supervising parks and golf courses, and working as sales representatives for agribusiness.

However, opportunities in research and other professional positions generally go to those with graduate degrees. Other employment opportunities include product development, teaching, extension work with governments (usually at the local level), regulatory work, and administrative positions. Working as a private contractor is a field that may be growing. A challenging recent area of work is integrated pest management—a field that encompasses the three pest categories for plants: plant pathology, entomology (study of insects), and weed sciences.

Typical employers of plant pathologists are the chemical and pesticide industries. Universities have teaching and research positions. The government at the state and federal levels also has positions—for example, in regulating plant trade across state lines. The Environmental Protection Agency and the Department of Agriculture hire plant pathologists. The larger agricultural states may have some positions for plant pathologists to work on problems facing the money crops: vegetables and fruits.

Plant Physiology

Plant physiologists study the way plants work. The science of plant physiology is dependent upon experiments for its knowledge. Basic research in plant physiology is simply an attempt to find answers—no benefit is necessary from this research. Applied research, however, attempts to solve problems faced in agriculture, forestry, or range management. The goal is to provide plants with the desired appearance that give the highest yield with the best nutritional value.

Some of the subfields of plant physiology deal with plant metabolism, or biochemistry; the movement of water through plants; the mineral nutrition required by plants for optimum growth; the growth and development of plants; plant response to environmental factors; and plant genetics.

In the past, plant physiologists have helped develop high-yield crops. Work continues on controlling plant pests, reducing the effect of stresses such as drought and high soil salinity, improving crop yields, and applying the study of hormones and growth regulators to plant growth and development. A newer, and still somewhat controversial, field is biotechnology, which involves genetic alteration of plants and crops to produce crops with desired characteristics, such as longer store shelf life; the changes may also actually include medicinal additions to established crops such as tomatoes. This work is almost entirely indoors, however, in the laboratories of biotechnology companies.

People who decide to be plant physiologists often do so because of a strong love of plants, gained from growing up on a farm or other activities during youth. Plant physiologists perform varied work. The specialty you choose will determine your work setting, which may be a biochemistry laboratory, greenhouse, lecture hall, mountaintop, plateau, apple orchard, or wheat field. A definite reward of plant physiology is the opportunity to serve humankind through advancing knowledge or solving problems faced by individuals working in agriculture, forestry, and range management.

Resource Management

All fifty states now have heritage programs. These are coordinated through the conservation organization The Nature Conservancy (see chapter 9 for more information on this organization) and employ field scientists to work in the field collecting data on ecosystems. Botanists work with these teams to inventory plants. Often these positions require advanced training.

ECOLOGY

Salary Range	Starting at about $24,500, averaging about $35,000, and reaching a top of about $43,000
Educational Requirements	College
Employment Outlook	Excellent

Ecology is the study of interactions among all types of life and, specifically, between an organism and its environment. *Interaction* is a key concept in the study of ecology. A variety of specialties are possible within the field. For example, an ecologist may study specific organisms, such as microbes, plants, animals, or humans, or certain types of habitat, such as fresh or marine waters or land. Others may study different theories, work on experiments, or research specific problems or methods of understanding an ecological system. While some of this study may take place outdoors, much of it will be done in libraries, in laboratories, or at computer terminals.

Ecologists need a solid knowledge of the sciences. Although biology will be the base, other necessary courses include mathematics, basic statistics, and computer science. Effective spoken and written communications are vital to ecologists, because financial support and action on problems may hinge on the way a problem or research need has been presented. Writing reports and analyses is also part of the job. Skill in communications, gained through coursework as well as practice, is essential for an ecologist.

The variety of positions in the field of ecology is tremendous. Most of these positions call for a specialization, such as aquatic ecology, wildlife ecology, or terrestrial ecology.

Ecologists find positions with consulting companies, industries, and the government. Other possibilities include teaching and research. Because of the increase in concern about our environment, the number of jobs for ecologists has increased. Competition is very keen for these openings, however, and top achievers with the best or most specific course background will have the edge.

See Profile, page 44.

VETERINARY MEDICINE

Salary Range	Starting at about $27,800, average about $63,000, and topping off at about $82,200
Educational Requirements	Advanced degree
Employment Outlook	Supply and demand are about equal, so previous work in a veterinary office will be an asset

Veterinarians today care for the health and well-being of animals and, indirectly, the people who own animals. Their education and training are quite rigorous and specifically aimed at the prevention, diagnosis, and treatment of animal health problems. Diagnosis will often involve tests, X rays, and the use of other equipment. Treatment may require setting a fracture, prescribing medication, delivering baby animals, or performing surgery.

In the United States well over half of all veterinarians work in private practice. They work on both ends of the health scale, preventing and treating disease and health problems. About half of these practitioners work with small animals, mostly pets such as cats and dogs. About 11 percent work with large animals—cattle, hogs, sheep, and horses. Many others have a mixed practice, which means they deal with both small and large animals.

The type of veterinary work that is most likely to involve working outdoors, often in inclement weather, is large-animal practice. Veterinarians treating farm and ranch animals also spend a fair amount of time driving to patients that cannot be brought into their offices.

Veterinarians also may teach others to assist with or provide veterinary services. Closely allied with teaching is research, in which veterinarians seek to prevent and find solutions to animal health problems. This research has also contributed directly to solutions for many human health problems. Veterinarians are employed in private industry for research and development, private testing and animal research, or marketing.

Two additional veterinary fields are regulatory medicine and public health. In regulatory medicine, veterinarians work to control or eradicate animal diseases and to protect the populace from those diseases that also affect humans. Public health work is performed for various branches of government and involves controlling diseases and promoting health.

Some veterinarians work in the military service, where they may be involved in biomedical or other research and development, food hygiene and safety, or treating government-owned animals. Others work in zoos and in aquatic animal medicine. A few work in space medicine and wildlife management. Other settings where veterinarians work include animal shelters, racetracks, fur ranches, and circuses.

To obtain a veterinary degree, seven years of college education must be completed: three years of preveterinary education and four years in a school of veterinary medicine.

A major reward of this career is the satisfaction of engaging in a respected profession that contributes to the health of society. The private practitioner also has the satisfaction of seeing sick animals recover and of assisting in keeping animals well. Self-employed private practitioners can set their own hours and work beyond normal retirement age. Their daily work may be quite varied and interesting. Veterinarians who work for the government, private firms, or colleges usually have pleasant working conditions, regular hours, and a steady income with good retirement programs and fringe benefits. Satisfaction from teaching or being involved in research programs is another reward of this career.

On the other hand, the hours for a new private practitioner can be long and irregular; the settings may be varied and possibly include dealing with bad weather. Bookwork, personnel, and other business matters are part of the details to work out in a private practice.

Some fields related to veterinary medicine are animal technology, animal husbandry, animal welfare, biological sciences, wildlife conservation, teaching, and research.

See Profile, page 46.

VETERINARY TECHNOLOGY

Salary Range:	Starting at about $15,000, averaging $25,000, and topping off at about $40,000
Educational Requirements	Some postsecondary studies
Employment Outlook	Good to above average

Veterinary technicians work in a variety of environments that include zoos, animal hospitals, and clinics assisting veterinarians, laboratories, or kennels. Most work with domestic animals, but some few are involved with exotic or endangered species. Although work with endangered species is scarce, it is very popular and therefore very competitive. Educational programs vary somewhat; some involve two and others four years of study.

A veterinary technician may spend up to 50 percent of the time in the laboratory, taking and developing X rays, testing for parasites, and examining samples taken from animals. Those who work in zoos will likely spend more time outdoors or in research to observe the animals in a native habitat. In rural areas a veterinary technician may assist a veterinarian in making farm calls to examine animals such as pigs, cows, horses, dogs, cats, sheep, mules, and chickens.

A veterinary technician will be trained on the job for the specific skills and procedures of that particular job. New graduates will know how to handle the usual species of animals treated and perform routine laboratory procedures. They will also be familiar with common drugs, instruments, and equipment.

ZOOLOGY

Salary Range	Starting between $20,000 and $25,000; with a master's degree, between $25,000 and $32,000; with a doctorate, between $35,000 and $40,000
Educational Requirements	Advanced degree
Employment Outlook	Good, especially with a doctorate

Zoology, the study of animals, is another broad field in the biological sciences. Zoology has many subfields dealing with all aspects of animal life, from microscopic cells to the study of a specific animal or interaction among animals. A zoologist may study the biology of a specific group of animals; for example, a herpetologist studies snakes, a mammalogist studies mammals, and a carcinologist studies crabs. Other specialties include the study of the structure of organisms (morphology), of fish (ichthyology), of birds (ornithology), of reptiles and amphibians (herpetology), of the function of organisms (physiology), and of how an organism develops and passes its characteristics on to another generation (developmental science).

If you want a career in this field, begin by studying the broad field of animal biology; you can enter a specialty when the area that's of most interest to you becomes clear. To allow for the most job opportunities in the field, it's wise to get a broad undergraduate background that includes courses in basic math, chemistry, and physics before concentrating too exclusively on an area of particular interest. To work in many fields, such as environmental science or marine biology, additional graduate training is required.

Academic institutions employ many animal biologists as teachers, researchers, or both. Teaching at the secondary level generally involves a broad knowledge of the field and includes teaching other science courses; a master's degree will add considerably to your knowledge and background and open up more possible jobs. College or university teaching requires specialization in one or more disciplines, and a doctorate is usually necessary for these positions.

Other possibilities for zoologists include museum work as a curator or setting up educational displays. Positions like this are very limited and are quite competitive, as are positions for zoologists in zoos. Industry offers a variety of opportunities in areas such as pollution reduction or pest control using biological agents. Jobs in pharmaceutical or chemical firms include sales and the testing of compounds.

Many federal government agencies hire zoologists, including the Public Health Service, the Fish and Wildlife Service, the National Park Service, the Department of Agriculture, the Food and Drug Administration, the Smithsonian Institution, and the National Academy of Sciences. State conservation commissions and fish and game commissions are other government employers of zoologists. Additional employment may be found as a science librarian or science writer.

Specialized training for individuals who wish to work in zoological parks or facilities for animals, particularly exotic species, is available at various facilities; an example is the Cat Tales Zoological Park in Spokane, Washington, whose combination of classroom work and hands-on training can give you an advantage in your job search. Career opportunities for which the park trains are: zookeeper, exotic animal handler, exotic animal trainer, environmental educator, and wildlife/conservation educator.

ANIMAL CARETAKING

Salary Range	Beginning at about $10,000, averaging about $14,000, and topping off at about $30,000
Educational Requirements	On-the-job training, although biology courses are an asset
Employment Outlook	Above average

Animal caretaking is an acknowledgment of the importance of animals to people. In our past, and continuing today, dogs have been used for hunting, cats to destroy rodents (which helped to end the bubonic plague), and caged birds to provide music. Other animals—horses and mules, elephants, camels, and cattle—have been used in farming or to carry burdens. More recently the pet industry, especially for domestic cats, dogs, ferrets, and birds, has grown rapidly and become increasingly important. Considering this growth, careers in animal caretaking have become even more important.

Animal caretakers are the individuals who feed and water, exercise, and nurture animals. They work in zoos, circuses, and amusement parks; in kennels, stables, shelters, and pet shops; with veterinarians; or in veterinary research.

In zoos, aquariums, circuses, and amusement parks, animal caretakers clean and maintain cages. They may need to transfer animals to other sites, and they arrange exhibits and set temperatures to maintain the animals' comfort. Their general responsibility is to ensure that the animals are in good health for public view.

Circuses and amusement parks also employ trainers to work with the animals and train them to perform certain stunts or tricks. Usually a trainer works with only one breed, such as lions, tigers, or elephants. Trainers are often involved in feeding, cleaning, and other maintenance tasks for the animals with which they work.

Kennel and shelter workers mostly care for small animals such as cats and dogs. They exercise animals, take them to rooms for treatment, check them carefully for signs of illness, and look to prevent dangerous situations in cages. In shelters the skilled animal attendants will put to death injured, ill, or unwanted animals and may administer vaccinations.

Stable workers run the gamut of work with horses: grooming, feeding and watering, saddling and unsaddling, rubbing down, and cooling off after riding. They also clean stalls and may, if they have a lot of experience, train horses.

Pet shop attendants care for the animals in pet shops. They feed and water, clean cages, and watch the animals carefully for any signs of an illness that could be contagious. They may even bathe dogs and cats and trim nails. Groomers may work with pet shops or have their own business. They mainly care for dogs, bathing and clipping to fit the standards of that particular breed.

Another career that involves working with animals and some outdoor work is pet sitting, a relatively new profession that has developed within the past twenty years. Pet sitting is attractive to individuals who love to work with animals and want to work out of their homes. Pet sitters take care of animals whose owners are away from home, and they flourish in large urban centers. Their services may include outdoor exercise for dogs. This is a career with great variations in demand; peaks come around traditional holiday seasons and during the summer.

A professional pet sitter does more than simply advertise a service. Quality standards are essential in this career. Pet Sitters International, a professional society, will help interested pet sitters develop their service to provide the best and most professional service possible. Pet sitting is a home-based business that requires minimal start-up capital; your greatest expenses are likely to be liability insurance and a dishonesty bond, which is recommended if you employ workers.

In some urban areas "doggie play groups" have been established. In these cases, individuals with outdoor space will take care of a number of dogs during the day in a situation that strongly resembles a day-care center for children.

Although no specialized training is required for working with animals, high school is a minimal requirement and biology courses are beneficial. Many aquariums, zoos, and circuses provide on-the-job training, but experience with animals can be a plus in obtaining these jobs. This experience can be gained through volunteer work at an animal shelter or by working for a veterinarian.

Zoos, aquariums, and amusement parks are becoming more popular, and some of the large zoos and parks are expanding. This means that there will continue to be positions that involve working with animals. In fact, as the move to provide better conditions for animals in these artificial environments continues, more jobs may open up for animal workers.

Animal caretakers interested in horses may find seasonal work at camps that offer horseback riding; the need for caretakers at public or private stables is also increasing.

Animal caretaking is a career that you can enter from volunteer work or from part-time work while still in high school. Volunteer work is especially useful to help you determine if you're truly interested in caretaking, and to learn about other possibilities that involve working with animals.

Animal caretaking is tied to the love affair that humans have with pets. As this love affair grows, so does the career of animal caretaker. The turnover rate among caretakers is fairly high, and advancement is totally dependent on the job setting. Your only promotions may be into management positions, which usually entail more deskwork and less work outside or with the animals.

A major plus of this work is the pleasure in working with animals. It can, however, be hard, dirty, and very repetitious—feeding and cleaning must take place every day, for example. It may also involve heavy lifting, and can be smelly and even dangerous. Many jobs also require more than a forty-hour work week.

See Profile, page 48.

ANIMAL TRAINING

Salary Range	Begins at about $10,500, averages about $26,000, and tops off at about $51,000
Educational Requirements	Some postsecondary study
Employment Outlook	Average to below average

Animal trainers teach animals to consistently behave in a certain manner. They work with show and race animals; with animals that perform in movies; and with guard, police, guide, or companion dogs. An animal trainer usually specializes in one or several types of animal. This is an old occupation; anthropology has unearthed evidence that ancient peoples trained dogs to help in the hunt, to herd or guard animals, and to provide protection.

Animal training is a slow and painstaking process of repetition and reward that teaches animals to perform on command. Training for the entertainment field—for motion pictures, circuses, or stage productions—may receive the most attention, but animals are trained for many other duties as well.

Many dogs are trained to assist in police work—handling unruly individuals, searching for missing people, or sniffing for illegal substances. Dogs are also trained to guard property, or to guide blind people, or to serve as companions and assistants that allow individuals with severe handicaps to live independently. In the latter situation, training may be required to help dog and owner work together as a team.

Horse trainers prepare horses for riding, for harness, and for show. The book and movie *The Horse Whisperer* deal with a style of training horses that has gained a great deal of attention in recent years. This method uses what founder Monty Roberts calls "the language of equus" to communicate with a horse and train it without the use of force. A specialty is racehorse training, which must be quite individual according to the needs of each animal.

To work as an animal trainer, you must like animals and be genuinely interested in working with them. Previous work with animals is essential; you can gain this through volunteer or part-time work or by advancing from the position of animal keeper to animal trainer. A three-year course of study prepares individuals for guide dog training. Other trainers find that study in animal psychology, in addition to previous work as a caretaker, is required.

The working hours and working conditions for animal trainers vary considerably and are totally dependent on what animal is being trained. Individuals who train aquatic mammals, such as dolphins and seals, must be comfortable working around, in, and under water. Trainers who work with wild animals, such as elephants or tigers, must always be careful. The chance that a previously tame animal suddenly will become dangerous is very real.

Animal trainers must be incredibly patient—the training routine, complete with rewards, must be repeated endlessly. Trainers must be able to show authority and keep the animals under their control while never displaying anger or punishing an animal that fails to perform a specific task.

Racehorse trainers receive the highest wages in this field, which usually includes a percentage of money won in races. If the horse is quite successful, this can provide a generous income. Show horse trainers may earn as much as $30,000 to $35,000 a year.

RESOURCES

Agricultural Research Service
U.S. Department of Agriculture
Agricultural Research Service
Personnel Division
Building 003, BARC-W
Beltsville, MD 20705
Telephone: 301-504-1317
Web: http://www.ars.usda.gov

Biological Sciences
American Institute of Biological Sciences
1444 Eye Street, NW, Suite 200
Washington, DC 20005
Telephone: 202-628-1500
Fax: 202-628-1509
Web: http://www.aibs.org

Botany
Botanical Society of America
American Journal of Botany
1735 Neil Avenue
Columbus, OH 43210
Telephone: 614-292-3519
Web: http://www.botany.org

Plant Pathology
The American Phytopathological Society
3340 Pilot Knob Road
St. Paul, MN 55121
Telephone: 612-454-7250
Fax: 612-454-0766
Web: http://www.scisoc.org

Plant Physiology
American Society of Plant Physiologists
15501 Monona Drive
Rockville, MD 20855-2768
Telephone: 301-251-0560

Fax: 301-279-2996
Web: http://www.aspp.org

Resource Management

The Nature Conservancy
Science Division
1815 North Lynn Street
Arlington, VA 22209
Telephone: 703-841-5300
Web: http://www.tnc.org
Jobs hot line: 703-247-3721

Ecology

The Ecological Society of America
2010 Massachusetts Avenue, NW, Suite 400
Washington, DC 20036
Telephone: 202-833-8773
Fax: 202-833-8775
Web: http://esa.sdsc.edu

Veterinary Medicine

American Veterinary Medical Association
1931 North Meacham Road, Suite 100
Schaumburg, IL 60173-4360
Telephone: 847-925-8070
Fax: 847-925-1329
Web: http://www.avma.org

American Association of Zoo Veterinarians
3400 West Girard Avenue
Philadelphia, PA 19104-1196
Telephone: 215-457-7027

Canadian Veterinary Medical Association
339 Booth Street
Ottawa, Ontario K1R 7K1
Telephone: 613-236-1162
Web: http://www.cvma-acmv.org/overview.htm

North American Veterinary Technician Association, Inc.
P.O. Box 224
Battle Ground, IN 47920
Telephone: 765-742-2216
Web: http://www.arma.org/navta/default.htm

Zoology

The Society for Integrative and Comparative Biology
401 North Michigan Avenue
Chicago, IL 60611-4267
Telephone: 312-527-6697 or 1-800-955-1236
Fax: 312-245-1085
Web: http://www.sicb.org

American Association of Zoo Keepers
635 South West Gage Boulevard
Topeka, KS 66606-2066
Telephone and fax: 785-273-1980
Web: http://aazk.epower.net

American Zoo and Aquarium Association
7970-D Old Georgetown Road
Bethesda, MD 20814-2493
Telephone: 301-562-0777
Web: http://www.aza.org

Cat Tales—Zoological Training Center
170720 North Newport Highway
Mead, WA 99021
Telephone: 509-238-4126
Web: http://www.zooschool.org/school.htm

Animal Caretakers

The American Humane Association
63 Inverness Drive East
Englewood, CO 80112
Telephone: 1-800-227-4645
Web: http://www.americanhumane.org

Humane Society of the United States
Companion Animals Division
2100 L Street, NW
Washington, DC 20037
Telephone: 202-452-1100
Fax: 202-778-6132
Web: http://www.hsus.org

The National Animal Control Association
806 South New York
Liberal, KS 67901
Telephone: 1-800-828-6474
Web: http://www.netplace.net/naca/default.htm

American Zoo and Aquarium Association
8403 Colesville Road, Suite 710
Silver Spring, MD 20910-3314
Telephone: 301-562-0777
Fax: 301-562-0888
Web: http://www.aza.org

Pet Sitters International
418 East King Street
King, NC 27021-9163
Telephone: 910-983-9222
Fax: 910-983-3755
Web: http://www.petsit.com

Profile

AQUATIC BIOLOGIST
Mark Hersh

Mark Hersh became an aquatic biologist because, he says, "I've always been interested in fishing and streams." Hersh's position with the Pennsylvania Department of Environmental Research is officially titled *water pollution biologist*, but he feels that *aquatic biologist* more accurately describes his work.

Hersh has a bachelor's degree in biology and an interdisciplinary master's in water resources. This is essential background for the job, in which he uses water chemistry and biological data to assess the health of an aquatic system. To ascertain the physical characteristics of a stream, he takes samples of the water (for chemical analysis) and of the fish. Plants, including the microscopic algae, insect forms, and other invertebrates are also studied.

"We collect data in summer and analyze it in winter, compiling it into a report," Hersh explains. "Sometimes we review reports done by private firms. I also spend time in meetings with, for example, persons seeking permits or representatives of the Environmental Protection Agency. We need to work with federal law and the programs delegated to the states."

Hersh says that any type of human activity relating to a body of water affects the biology of the water. He often investigates pollution spills or fish kills. "Sometimes we study individual organisms and other times the whole system. Then we recommend the level of protection the stream should get. I must know what to expect in any system so I can find out if it is disturbed or not and what the human impact has been. Cause-and-effect relationships are elusive."

In addition to his specialized knowledge, Hersh needs to know taxonomy and must be able to use reference materials. Writing skills are also important for the numerous reports he must prepare. Another essential skill for an aquatic biologist is the ability to work with people. On his job, Hersh deals with other professionals, the public, and information specialists.

The mix of indoor-outdoor work for aquatic biologists depends on the position and the season. "In the summer I spend 60 to 80 percent of my time outside in good weather, " Hersh says. "Some will spend a majority of their time outdoors, and others none at all. As you advance up the career ladder, you get less outdoor work.

"We call ourselves 'windshield surveyors' because our responsibility encompasses the whole state. We may spend more time getting to the location than we spend in the stream," he comments wryly.

Patience with bureaucracy is a desirable personality trait for Hersh's position. "It is also important to derive satisfaction from doing your job and doing it well," he acknowledges realistically, "because the monetary rewards are not that great."

What is Hersh's advice for someone interested in becoming an aquatic biologist? "Question your motives. Ask yourself why you want to do this. Don't do this if you think it consists of walking through woods looking at pretty streams. Before you get into this career, make sure it is what you want to do.

"If you want to be an environmental activist, there are other ways to accomplish the same ends. This is a field where citizen activists can make a difference. Activism pays more and allows you to live anywhere. Volunteering may allow you to have the same or greater impact. Trout Unlimited is one group with knowledgeable laypeople."

Hersh mentions that some negatives of his job include limited opportunities and potential for advancement. Also, he says, "The job you want might not be in a great geographic location."

But his job does have its advantages. "With government work there is no client to please. And I like streams as a system. It is a big puzzle to try to work out."

See Aquatic Biology, page 25.

Profile

ECOLOGIST
Rebecca Sharitz

"Ecologists need to have a strong curiosity about the functioning of natural systems," Rebecca Sharitz declares. "In some areas of ecology, it also helps to be enthusiastic about outdoor activities and not mind being occasionally muddy, dirty, uncomfortable, and wet."

Sharitz should know. She is a professor of ecology in the department of botany at the University of Georgia and spends a major part of her time at the University's Savannah River Ecology Laboratory (SREL). There she is senior research ecologist and the head of the Division of Wetlands Ecology, directing a $2.8 million program that employs seven Ph.D.s and several postdoctoral fellows. She also supervises the research activities of a number of graduate students.

Her decision to enter the field of ecology was strongly influenced by her youth on a rural Virginia farm, her desire to do research in an outdoor environment, and the contagious enthusiasm of the professor of her first college ecology course. She has a bachelor's degree in biology and a doctorate in botany with a major in ecology.

Sharitz conducts research to determine the effects of human activities on forest wetland habitats, such as those along the major rivers in the southeastern United States. "By changing the flood patterns of rivers through construction of dams and reservoirs we impact adjacent swamps and floodplain forests," Sharitz explains. "I study the effects of these man-made changes on the population biology of wetland plants." She has been working at several research sites along the Savannah River for more than twenty years. "To evaluate the effects of human activities on the environment, we must understand natural ecological processes. So, much of my research is also on undisturbed populations of wetland plants."

Since Hurricane Hugo slashed through the eastern United States in 1989, Sharitz has also conducted research in the Congaree Swamp National Monument in South Carolina, a wilderness area of the national park system. Here she studies the degree of disturbance and the timing of recovery from the effects of Hugo on the bottomland hardwood forests. This study of the effects of a natural event—the hurricane—complements her research on human impact on the environment.

Sharitz says there is no such thing as a typical day or week on her job. One recent week found her spending two days at the University of Georgia, although she normally visits the campus only once a week, devoting the greatest amount of her time to research at the SREL. On Monday she attended the final seminar of one of her Ph.D. students. On Tuesday she taught a course. Wednesday was spent in her research office at SREL, writing a scientific paper, reviewing manuscripts, and meeting with students and other researchers. Thursday she was in the Congaree Swamp from dawn until dusk, mapping and measuring trees to check their recovery from the hurricane. On Friday she analyzed data and tended to various types of administrative paperwork.

Ideal preparation for a career in ecology, according to Sharitz, should include a broad background in biology and chemistry in addition to ecology. "Don't narrow your focus too early in your academic studies, but build a broad base of knowledge," she emphasizes. "For my field a good understanding of natural history—plants, animals, soils, and geology—is important." Solid training in statistics and in mathematics, as well as a facility with a variety of computer programs, can be extremely valuable.

"Writing is another critical skill," she adds. "You must be able to communicate the results of your research effectively. Speaking skills are also important for expressing ideas at scientific meetings and for teaching." Depending on the specific research interests of an ecologist, certain foreign language skills can be an asset. Foreign languages may be necessary for conducting research in other countries.

According to Sharitz, the greatest number of ecology positions today appear to be in environmental consulting, with industries, or with state and local governments. For these positions a master's degree is becoming a necessity. Academic positions in ecology, which require a doctorate, seem to be dwindling.

The aspects of her job that Sharitz enjoys most are working outdoors and working with other outdoorspeople, although she admits ruefully that she used to spend more time out in the field than she can now. Her job now requires that she spend a lot of time preparing reports and doing paperwork involved with quality control and compliance with governmental regulations. "These activities may be important, but they do take the scientist's time away from the actual science," she says.

See Ecology, page 30.

Profile
VETERINARIAN
Donna Matthews

"As a kid I always wanted to be a vet, and I started working with a vet after school when I was sixteen," says Donna Matthews, a veterinarian in Luray, Virginia. Nevertheless, she found it difficult to translate her childhood dream into reality. As a college freshman she applied to veterinary school but was refused admission—in the early 1970s veterinary schools accepted few women. This pattern persisted throughout her four years of college, and after graduating with a bachelor's degree in animal science, she worked at a sheep farm run by the National Institutes of Health. Ten years after her first application, Matthews finally gained admission to veterinary school. She says that now veterinary school classes are about half male and half female.

Matthews specializes in small ruminants—sheep and llamas—although her practice includes other animals. Llamas, says Matthews, are good animals for the farmer who doesn't want to invest a lot of money and equipment in farming; quite a lot of them are raised in her area. "Llamas have a lot of personality, their babies are incredible, and the people who raise them are very interesting," she says enthusiastically. "Because we in North America don't know a lot about llamas, we are breaking new ground as we deal with them. It's quite a challenge."

Matthews spends from half to three-quarters of her time outdoors. She begins a typical day in her clinic, examining hospitalized patients and taking in-clinic appointments. By late morning she is outdoors, where she stays until late afternoon when she returns to the clinic. She says, however, that her schedule is not at all typical of other outdoor veterinarians: "There are many different outside vets and each one does it differently."

In her outdoor visits she checks to see how many animals are pregnant and if the males are fertile. She also keeps her outdoor patients on a careful health regimen that includes regular vaccinations.

"My job is very challenging and at times very rewarding. On pretty days there is nothing better than playing outside with sheep on a farm." Matthews says that scheduling her visits to Luray-area farms can be a real challenge.

She admits candidly that there are many things she doesn't like about her career. "The lifestyle is terrible. I am on call continually—my clients don't accept other vets but want me to attend to problems. I also have to be all things to all people at all times—I have to work with every system on every creature even though I am more comfortable in my specialty." She concedes, however, that this is probably more typical of a rural veterinary practice than an urban one.

She adds: "To stay with this career you must really want to do it. The pay is not equal to almost any other career for which you spend this amount of time in preparation. Because the thing I enjoy most about my work is the medicine, I often think I should have gone to medical school." Had she done so, she believes her compensation would be more in line with the time she spent training for her career.

Contrary to many expectations, veterinary work is very people intensive, Matthews notes. "People sometimes say to me, 'I want to be a vet because I just want to work with animals.' This is a misconception. I spend a great deal of my time dealing with people, not just working with animals."

Matthews suggests that a broad background in undergraduate studies, not simply a focus on science, is the best preparation for veterinary school, which takes four years.

Her advice to would-be vets: "Make sure you really want to get into this career. Spend time with a practitioner seeing how much work it is and how much of a total commitment it really is."

See Veterinary Medicine, page 31.

Profile

ELEPHANT TRAINER
April Yoder

"Lady, leave it!" Elephant trainer April Yoder speaks firmly and carries a small stick. Beside the elephants, the five-foot-six Yoder looks diminutive. "When you give a command, you have to sound authoritative," she says. "You can say it very softly as long as you say it with authority."

Her enthusiasm for her job is obvious. "I love working with the elephants. Each one has a different personality, and I like to be able to get close to them and develop a relationship with them. They're very challenging animals. They have such excellent memories and are so intelligent."

Yoder's route to her present job was just a few short steps from her graduation with a bachelor of science in biology. She says that although she has always loved animals, she didn't major in zoology because she thought it was too specific. She felt that a biology major would give her more opportunities and enable her to go in many directions.

"I always knew I would work with animals," Yoder relates. "I didn't want to work in a lab or inside because I'm an outdoors-type person. Despite my degree, I wasn't sure where I would be able to find a job, because I had zero experience. So when I found a ten-month seasonal position here, I was ecstatic—it was everything I had ever dreamed of!"

Yoder has been with the elephants at Kings Dominion Park near Richmond, Virginia, for two years now. She says that seasonal employment is a good way to start. Or better yet, she suggests, become a seasonal volunteer so that you will have a chance to closely observe the elephants. Elephants sometimes do not like certain people, and seasonal work can give you a feel for whether this is what you want to do.

Asked what advice she'd give someone who wants to be an elephant trainer, Yoder responds without hesitation, "I'd tell them to go for it!" She then adds thoughtfully, "I'd tell them to think about it, because it's not something you can do for two months and then say, 'That's it.' The animals get used to you. You really have to make sure it's what you want to do."

About developing the important relationship between elephant and trainer, Yoder explains, "You get used to them at the same time they're getting used to you. When I first started working with elephants, I was absolutely petrified. I didn't really realize their size until I was right up on them.

"In this job you have to be very dedicated because the elephants require so much work. You have to put yourself wholeheartedly into it. And you have to pump yourself up when you walk into the barn to impress on them that you're in charge. It's called 'the elephant attitude.'"

Kings Dominion has two senior elephant handlers, with a third in training. For her first five months Yoder worked as a junior, giving basic commands to the elephants. Her lucky break came with a staff turnover. After a month of intensive coaching (eight hours a day, five or six days a week) by noted movie-animal trainer David McMillan, she became a senior handler.

Her daily routine begins with a morning check to be sure the elephants are okay. At night they are loose in the barn, but they are placed in chains for their morning feeding. In the summer they spend their days on Elephant Island, and in cooler weather they stay indoors.

"In the evening we bring them in and feed them, again in chains, then put them in the barn and let them loose. That's their day. Of course, we have to clean up—that's the best part," Yoder jokes. Other duties include "maintaining the exhibits, cutting the grass, fixing whatever breaks, carpentry work, and landscaping work. Most people here are jacks-of-all-trades."

In the spring, summer, and fall Yoder spends four or five hours outdoors with the elephants, which she says is not enough. "During the wintertime we spend more time with them because they are here in the barn."

Yoder admits that one drawback of working with elephants is their unpredictability. "These guys are very docile. But elephants are the number one reason for deaths in zoos because of their size. They are so dangerous and unpredictable. Sometimes it's accidental, but not always. So when you're in the barn, you always have to be aware of where they are and what they're doing. That's why I carry the ankus stick around—for safety reasons." It's also why only designated elephant handlers are allowed to work with the elephants. Seasonals normally take care of the giraffes and white rhinos but have limited contact with the elephants, although they help take care of the elephant barn. "We have very strict rules because of the danger."

The only real downside of her job, Yoder confides, is that taking care of elephants can be very frustrating. "Yesterday was a perfect example. I got so frustrated because they wouldn't eat, and I worried about them. It's like a mother when her children are sick. Sometimes they can be like two-year-old children: You can do everything and they won't listen to you. And it's very hard to keep calm. It's a discipline you have to acquire."

How do you prepare to become an elephant handler? "All of the elephant work I do I basically learned hands-on," answers Yoder. "But my biology degree does help, because when I talk with the vet about medical problems, I can understand what she's saying. I'm more aware of what's going on because of having been taught about the scientific method of how to do research."

Yoder expects to stay with the elephants for a while longer. "Two years is not a lot of experience in some people's eyes; a lot of handlers have tended two years." Gaining additional experience will serve her well, she believes. Though not yet certain about her career path, Yoder sees the possibility of having her own facility. Management has less appeal, because it would mean spending little time with the elephants themselves.

See Animal Caretaking, page 35.

Chapter 4

Conservation

We won't have a society if we destroy the environment.
                                        Margaret Mead

Conservation is generally defined as "the management, preservation, and careful use of natural resources—air, water, soil, minerals, plants, and animals—for economic or recreational purposes." The need for conservation in the United States did not become apparent to many until the late nineteenth century. At that time the move to conserve natural resources was largely a response to the flagrant killing of North American wildlife such as the beaver and the buffalo.

Prominent American naturalists—notably John James Audubon, Henry David Thoreau, George Perkins Marsh, and John Muir—had promoted the ideas of conservation as early as the 1850s. The first national park in the world, Yellowstone, was established in 1872.

Conservation gained status as a national movement in the early 1900s. Under the presidency of Theodore Roosevelt, who was greatly interested in conservation issues, the first federal wildlife refuge—Pelican Island, Florida—was established in 1903, and more than 140 million acres were added to the national forest reserves.

An impetus to this emerging movement came when a major White House conference attended by governors, federal officials, scientists, business executives, and conservationists was held in 1908. Convened to set national conservation policies, this conference resulted in the decision to use public lands for purposes other than commercial development.

Another far-reaching outcome was the establishment soon afterward of conservation commissions in forty-one states.

The term *conservation* was apparently first used by Gifford Pinchot, the head of the U.S. Forest Service during Theodore Roosevelt's administration. Early efforts at conservation centered on preserving forests and wildlife. The need for soil conservation was dramatized in the early 1930s when the disaster generally known as the Dust Bowl hit the Great Plains. During this time, windstorms blew away the fertile topsoil, which had been damaged by poor farming and ranching practices and a prolonged drought. Because of this disastrous experience, the term *conservation* now encompasses soil science in addition to forestry and wildlife biology.

Careers related to conservation are many and varied. They generally involve management of and education about resources. Landscaping careers increasingly relate to conservation, and they are also covered in this chapter.

PARK MANAGEMENT

Salary Range	Varies with employer; with the U.S. Park Service, rangers make between $18,500 and $42,000, interpreters between $19,000 and $29,000
Educational Requirements	Some park ranger positions require only a two-year associate's degree; for other positions, including interpretation, a bachelor's degree is a minimal requirement
Employment Outlook	Little or slower-than-average growth

Park management work in the U.S. western national parks was originally performed by U.S. Army troops. Civilian park rangers replaced the troops when the National Park Service was formed in 1916. The image of the park ranger has changed in recent years; it no longer is that of a person whose noble and generous character has been shaped by long periods in the remote outdoor reaches of a large wilderness park. With the creation of more urban parks, and following the 1970 riots in Yosemite, more emphasis has had to be placed on law enforcement. Additionally, the ecological impacts of all actions are now of more concern to rangers.

The majority of park ranger positions are with the federal government through the National Park Service, a bureau of the U.S. Department of the

Interior. State and county parks also provide job possibilities for park rangers, although they may not be as large or as well staffed as their federal counterparts. Additionally, there are many privately owned and operated parks, such as the historical parks at Colonial Williamsburg, Old Sturbridge Village, and Monticello, the home of Thomas Jefferson.

The U.S. National Park Service

The National Park Service oversees the National Park System. Four basic types of parks exist: natural, cultural, historical, and recreational. Some parks, of course, have more than one of these functions. There are about 321 parks and about seventy-seven million acres of national parkland in forty-nine states (all but Delaware), plus Puerto Rico, Guam, and the Virgin Islands. The two main goals of the park service are to save the natural and cultural resources of the country and to give the public access to recreational, inspirational, and educational experiences.

More than half of all park rangers in the United States work in areas east of the Mississippi River. While much of their work is conducted in the outdoors, office work is also necessary. As rangers advance into managerial positions, they spend more and more time indoors in meetings, writing reports, and performing other managerial tasks.

Four types of jobs are held by park rangers: historical interpretation, natural interpretation, resource management, and law enforcement. The exact tasks of each ranger position will depend on the type of job and the park. Not all parks have all of these positions. For example, the National Capital Region in Washington, D.C., has few full-time law enforcement positions, because the park police provide this service. Parks in other regions do have law enforcement positions. The type of park also influences the variety of positions available. Some parks—such as Yosemite, Yellowstone, and Mesa Verde—are like small cities, and park ranger positions in these parks include functions such as sewer maintenance and fire management.

Competition for park ranger positions is very keen, and these jobs are difficult to obtain. One strategy is to stay aware of jobs available at the park or parks in which you are interested by visiting the U.S. government's official Web site for jobs and employment information, which is provided by the U.S. Office of Personnel Management. (See the Resources section of this chapter.)

Park Resource Management

A park ranger in charge of resource management has an incredible variety of tasks. These often involve interaction with people living or owning land near the park. For example, one responsibility of a resource manager is to control infestations, such as of gypsy moths. Rangers patrol the park area looking for evidence of gypsy moths; egg masses on trees is typical evidence of the presence of gypsy moths. If rangers determine that the area needs to be sprayed, adjacent landowners must be notified in advance of the spraying. Duties also include keeping walking trails in good shape for hikers and dealing with other issues relating to park resources as they arise.

In addition to knowledge about natural resources, a park ranger in charge of resource management needs people skills, because there is constant interaction with users of the park and contact with adjacent landowners. Excellent verbal communication skills are essential, as are writing skills for handling reports and other necessary communications.

See Profile, page 70.

Interpretation

Interpreters, or naturalists, are responsible for communicating information about nature and the environment through talks, tours, museum displays, or newsletters. Some interpreters are classified as park rangers in national or other large parks.

Interpreters come from several academic backgrounds: natural resources, such as biology, forestry, or soils; education; and history. Communications courses are important background for writing press releases, reports, and brochures; for working with the public; and for working with the electronic media. Computer literacy and administrative skills are also important qualifications.

Although the work settings and employers are quite varied, most interpreters are employed by parks and recreation areas, museums, educational settings, and organizations concerned with different aspects of the environment. The educational background required for interpretation jobs varies according to the position, but a bachelor's degree is usually necessary, and advanced degrees may be required for some levels of work. Parks and recreation areas have many seasonal (usually summer) interpretation jobs. Seasonal or internship positions are typical first jobs for naturalist interpreters. In fact, many work in these types of positions for years, going from one seasonal job to another.

Interpretive naturalist positions, especially with the government, are strongly influenced by the economic climate. Because the field is recent, these jobs are often the first to be dropped when money is scarce and the government begins to tighten its spending.

See Profile, page 71.

FISH AND WILDLIFE MANAGEMENT

Salary Range	Varies widely, depending on employer, but generally between $18,500 and $40,000, depending on experience, location, and job responsibilities
Educational Requirements	Master's degree for the best opportunities
Employment Outlook	Jobs are expected to increase at a slow rate

The fish and wildlife manager is one of a number of professional resource managers; others are forest rangers, park naturalists, and range managers. The term *wildlife* applies to animals that are not domesticated. The fish and wildlife manager is often interested in game animals harvested for food or sport. Management of nongame species, such as songbirds and small animals, is also a concern. Although fish are technically a type of wildlife, they are often placed in a separate category because their habitat is so different. Both fish and their habitat are managed by the fish and wildlife manager.

The fish and wildlife manager needs to ensure that populations of wildlife are maintained at satisfactory levels. The job entails gathering data through research in the field and applying scientific solutions to problems facing a particular species. It may also involve habitat maintenance. Enforcement of regulations controlling hunting and fishing seasons is another of the responsibilities of this manager.

A very important part of the work of the fish and wildlife manager is education. Informing others about the management and ecology of wildlife through work at a nature or conservation center is essential for the future of wildlife.

Background for fish and wildlife management should include general science courses—such as botany, zoology, ecology, hydrology, and geology—plus social sciences and communications courses. It is particularly helpful if one or more courses are taken at a field or biological station so you can experience actual fieldwork.

A bachelor's degree in wildlife management or fisheries science may lead to only part-time or temporary jobs in the field. A master's degree is now becoming essential for a career in this field; most of the jobs advertised call for one. A master's degree usually leads to a job managing resources or to an administrative position. A doctorate is essential for university teaching, research positions, or consulting work.

The government is the major employer of fish and wildlife managers. State conservation agencies and federal government departments, such as the Fish and Wildlife Service, are the primary departments providing work. Some city and county governments in high population areas also need specialists. Jobs with private industries and management positions also exist. Positions in teaching and research are available for those with graduate level training.

See Profile, page 73.

FOREST MANAGEMENT

Salary Range	Starts at about $18,000, averages about $35,000, and tops out at about $75,000; forest technicians generally earn between $16,000 and $28,500
Educational Requirements	Foresters need a minimum of a bachelor's degree, a master's for research, and a master's or doctorate for teaching; forest technicians need high school plus on-the-job training or a two-year technician's degree
Employment Outlook	Below average

Forestry work involves managing and using forests and related natural resources to benefit humans. This requires knowledge of soil, air, water, trees and other plants, wild and domestic animals, and the interrelationships among all these factors.

Working with people and issues related to public land use is also part of forest management. The abilities to relate well to people and problem solve are essential for this career. Two of the more common positions in forest management are forester and forest technician.

The U.S. Forest Service

The U.S. Forest Service, a part of the Department of Agriculture, is undoubtedly the single largest employer of foresters and forest technicians in the United States. The government has more positions for forestry technicians than for foresters. Some people who have the necessary qualifications for forester positions take technician positions; a limited number of these later move into positions as foresters.

A typical career path with the forest service starts with work as a seasonal employee before obtaining a permanent job. Administrative positions in the forest service are, in ascending order, district ranger, forester, forest supervisor, and chief of forest service.

If you're interested in becoming a district ranger, you must compete for the job. If you don't want to perform the administrative work of a district ranger, other types of positions at the same grade level are available. These are specialty positions involving, for instance, work with timber, recreation, wildlife, or engineering. Higher grades include positions as supervisors in regional offices or in the Washington office. Professionals in the forest service have opportunities to move around. There is, in fact, a mobility policy within the agency: people move to get promotions.

The forest service is experiencing a steady number of retirements in forestry positions that will continue until 2002. Although this should open up some jobs, the number of these positions may be declining because of concerns over the cutting of old-growth forests and economic problems. While the forest service has many positions for wildlife biologists, fisheries biologists, and law enforcement personnel, forester and forest technician jobs are also advertised.

Forestry

Some of the duties a forester performs include planting, measuring, and grading trees; supervising timber harvests; developing plans for recreation areas; cooperating with states to manage wildlife habitats (for big game, small game, and fish); planning to ensure an abundance of wildlife; managing watersheds for flood control, timber production, and soil conservation; evaluating and managing insect and disease outbreaks; and planning roads and trails.

A college degree, with strong emphasis on science and math, is important for forestry work. Forestry curricula at the accredited forestry schools in the United States concentrate on the biological, physical, and social sciences. Increasingly, however, they have been emphasizing sociology and psychology. The ability to work with others in group situations, in problem solving, and for marketing is essential, especially for people in management positions. Writing and public speaking courses are also important background for forester positions.

A recent position listing with the U.S. Forest Service highlighted "extensive contact with private landowners, representatives of forest industry and government agencies, and the general public." It further stated: "Selectees can expect to be on overnight travel 50 to 100 percent of the time, often to remote and isolated locations."

Entry-level forestry jobs are very competitive, and graduates with top marks will have an advantage in job hunting. Summer work experience in a forestry job will also be a plus. It is government policy that the various agency workforces should have percentages of minorities and women similar to those in the civilian labor force. Although the number of women in forestry has increased in recent years, both the government and private organizations are recruiting more minorities for forestry projects.

Foresters often advance from hands-on, outdoor, entry-level positions to administrative positions largely performed indoors. Administrators oversee organizational work, planning, budget preparation and management, report preparation, and contracting.

One reason forestry positions are attractive is the opportunity to be immersed in the natural environment. Still, although many foresters live and work in rural settings, numerous positions for foresters are also available in or near large urban areas.

Foresters find jobs in municipal, county, state, and federal settings. Other positions are available in universities and schools, with industrial associations, and for citizens' organizations. Management positions exist in conservation organizations, public agencies involved in land management, and private industries such as forest-products companies. Some people also work as private consulting foresters.

See Profile, page 74.

Forest Technology

Work performed by forest technicians is markedly similar to that of the forester, but technicians usually work as part of a team under the supervision of foresters. In contrast, foresters work in management and planning, and apply their training to the task at hand. Both pay and possibilities for career advancement are lower for forest technicians than for foresters.

Technicians do, however, work mainly in the outdoors. A major task is to collect data. This includes measuring and recording tree height and diameter, and recording rain gauge data. Technicians also perform tasks such as thinning young stands of timber to improve productivity, maintaining public camping areas, and working as firefighters or on fire lookout duty. Forest technician work has evolved into more complicated work with many different types of activities.

Forest technicians must have a college degree. They also may be required to work with the visitors to a park, giving information about recreation opportunities, fire prevention, safety in the park, and sanitary and other regulations. Technicians may also inspect recreation areas to monitor adherence to laws and regulations and inform visitors of violations.

CONSERVATION DISTRICT WORK

Salary Range	Administrative positions from $48,000 to $57,000; technical (depending on education and job requirements), $28,000 to $42,000; clerical, $22,000 to $28,000; public information, $25,000 to $32,000
Educational Requirements	Depend on the complexity of the job; some positions require a master's degree or doctorate
Employment Outlook	Poor due to financial problems facing states and counties, but not lack of need

Under the general umbrella of the U.S. Department of Agriculture, the country is organized into nearly three thousand conservation districts—almost one for every county—that deal with conservation issues for private land. These districts help each local area in conserving resources such as water, land, wildlife, forests, and other natural resources. Across the country their names vary—for example, they may be called soil and water conservation districts, resource conservation districts, natural resource districts, or the like. Whatever the name of the local district, the mission, as defined on the National Association of County Districts' Web page, is: "To coordinate assistance from all available sources—public and private, local, state and federal—in an effort to develop locally driven solutions to natural resource concerns."

Conservation districts were established in 1937 in response to the great Dust Bowl disaster. The original focus, understandably, was on soil conservation. They have met with a fair amount of success since their founding, and the current mandate of the conservation districts has broadened to include protection of all earth-based resources: soil, water, and wetlands. New challenges faced by these districts include irrigation and flood protection; threats to plant and animal habitat and water quality posed by urban expansion; construction practices that accelerate erosion and allow sediment to leach into waterways; and excessive fertilizer and pesticide use by homeowners that also pollutes local groundwater. Conservation districts help developers and homeowners relate to their land in an environmentally sensitive manner, work to educate communities and students about the value of natural resources, and encourage local conservation efforts.

A key function of these districts is planning, both annual and long range. These plans become a program that identifies opportunities to develop and conserve local natural resources. The districts may also be charged with following through on state legislation, such as the Chesapeake Bay Preservation Act passed by the state of Virginia. This act requires conservation plans to protect the Chesapeake Bay, and the appropriate districts review these plans to see if they will fulfill this function.

Sometimes one conservation district office is in charge of several counties, with only one staff member or a part-time clerical person employed. Urban areas that have more problems usually have larger offices. For example, the office that covers Fairfax County, Virginia—Northern Virginia Soil and Water Conservation District—employs full-time staffers to fill positions that involve extensive outdoor work and training in fields such as conservation engineering, earth science, agronomy, and soil science.

Unfortunately, salaries in these offices are not usually competitive with jobs in industry. They do, however, offer conservation jobs, good experience, and second careers for retired civil servants.

The district movement is founded on grassroots voluntarism, and many opportunities exist for volunteers to get involved. Volunteers may be high school or college students or retirees—anyone who wants to spend some free time working to help the environment. Volunteering with these districts is a good way to learn about them and about environmentally oriented work.

Locating local districts can be a challenge; many do not have a separate telephone number but are listed under the Soil Conservation Service of the U.S. Department of Agriculture. If you can't find the number in the government pages of your telephone directory, the Web site of the National Association of Conservation Districts has a link to a state-by-state listing. See the Resources section at the end of this chapter for the Web address and other information.

HORTICULTURAL TECHNOLOGY

Salary Range	Beginning salaries are about $12,400, average about $25,000, and top about $45,000
Educational Requirements	A combination of postsecondary and on-the-job training
Employment Outlook	Good for arborists; landscape positions are generally cut back in an economic slowdown

Keeping gardens is not a new art; it dates back to the famous hanging gardens of Babylon, the tulips of Holland, and the formal gardens of France's royal palaces. As the nature of work has changed over the years and individuals have found themselves with increased leisure time, parks, flowers, and gardens have become more important. This has begun to increase the need for trained horticultural technicians.

The role of horticultural technicians is to improve and protect the gifts of nature to provide a better environment for humans. Horticultural technicians usually have a specialty in at least one of these areas: flowers (floriculture); shrubs, hedges, and trees (nursery operation); grass (turf grass); trees (arborist); and landscape development. These technicians work with public as well as private lands, including parks, playgrounds, and the shoulders of public highways.

Technicians who work in floriculture and in nursery operations perform very similar activities and often will do both jobs. Both types of technicians work in nurseries and are involved in raising and selling plants. Both of these positions also involve mostly indoor work.

More outdoor work is involved in work with turf grass, trees, and landscape development. Turf grass technicians usually work in one of these areas: maintaining commercial lands and construction sites; planning and maintaining public lands, such as parks, highways, and playing fields; and related areas such as producing sod and seeds, irrigation, transportation, and sales of related products and services. They find work with private companies or own their own businesses, often providing complete lawn maintenance from fertilizing and mowing to controlling pests, disease, and weeds. Public-sector work can be found at all levels of government and often involves planning areas in parks or playing fields that get very hard usage.

Some individuals work in sports stadiums; whether they're of natural grass or artificial turf, the stadium grounds demand a fair amount of work.

There are two concerns: functional grounds for the sport of the season and attractive grounds for the enjoyment of the public. During sports seasons the job can demand long days, but many find it extremely interesting and rewarding work. Others manage the turf at golf courses.

People who work in arboriculture (arborists) also do more of their work outdoors as they take care of trees and shrubs in the urban environment. The work includes selecting and planting the proper types of trees for a particular space, correctly placing and removing trees, pruning, fertilizing, and controlling pests.

An arborist must have good health and physical stamina, as well as the ability to function as part of a team. The work often involves using heavy equipment or equipment that demands manual dexterity and coordination, although the basic work of the arborist is done by hand. Some of the work—for example, pruning trees—is done above the ground, and good balance is required.

Arborists generally find employment in a private company; in the public sector working with parks; in an arboretum; or with agencies that care for highways, monuments, or buildings. They may also work as landscapers or grounds managers. This is an expanding field with opportunities at all levels of employment.

If you're interested in horticultural technology, you can take advantage of a variety of educational opportunities, including vocational courses in secondary school and two-year programs following high school. These often include some training in the field or related work experience. Going from part-time or summer work to full-time work is one route into this career. It is possible, too, to learn on the job and work upward through the ranks as your knowledge and skills grow.

LANDSCAPE ARCHITECTURE

Salary Range	Starting at about $17,000, averaging $50,000, and topping off in the $100,000-plus range
Educational Requirements	Four- to five-year bachelor's degree
Employment Outlook	Average; positions are cut back in a poor economy

The focus for a landscape architect is the relation of people to the environment. Although this has been a recognized profession for the past hundred years, the increased environmental awareness since the 1960s has helped the field expand. Landscape architects encourage protection of natural resources while they work to provide for the increased housing and recreation needs of the public. Designing public areas—parks, campuses, shopping centers, and industrial parks—so that they are beautiful as well as functional is the major task of landscape architects. In doing this, the landscape architect often works as part of a team that includes architects, engineers, planners, and horticulturists.

Traditionally, landscape architects designed parks and gardens; today that is just one specialty of the profession. Others include landscape designing for hotels and resorts, shopping centers, and public or private housing. Some landscape architects prepare studies on cost, environmental impact, and feasibility or are involved in regional planning and resource management. Some not only design but also supervise site work. Other landscape architects have been involved in developing streets, bypasses, and parkways.

Working time is usually balanced between the indoors and outdoors: Part of the time is spent in the office preparing drawings and models, and discussing these and cost estimates with clients. The rest of the time is spent outdoors studying and planning the sites and supervising the projects. Necessary personal qualities of landscape architects include an appreciation of nature, creativity, and artistic talent.

The minimum educational requirement is a bachelor's degree in landscaping design. High school courses that provide important background include mechanical or geometrical drawing, art, botany, and mathematics. Facility in written and spoken English is important for making group presentations and writing project proposals. Technical courses in college include surveying, graphics, structural design, and landscape design and construction. Also required are courses in horticulture and botany, planning, science, mathematics, English, and the social sciences.

Although this is a promising field, its growth is tied to construction growth, which is determined by the economy. When construction is slow, the demand for landscape architects is reduced. During the 1980s, a boom period, work for landscape architects was plentiful. With the recession of the early 1990s, the situation changed. Although more construction has been taking place at the end of the 1990s, the outlook for this career in the near future is not yet clear.

See Profile, page 76.

SEASONAL AND VOLUNTEER WORK

The conservation field is an area that offers a wide variety of seasonal and volunteer employment. These positions provide experience and knowledge of the field, and they may also lead to full-time positions. See the Resources section for a listing of contacts for park volunteer jobs.

The National Park System

Many people use seasonal work as a means to get into full-time employment with the National Park System. To do this successfully, it is advantageous to work in several different parks to get a wide range of experience and also get to know a number of individuals employed in the park system.

When seasonal work peaks during the summer months, somewhere in the neighborhood of fourteen thousand summer, part-time, and temporary employees work in national parks. These jobs are very competitive, especially those in the larger parks, and the number of applicants is far greater than the number of positions available. Obtaining seasonal positions in the smaller parks or in winter is easier. Applicants with previous seasonal park experience, special skills applicable in a certain setting (a history background for a historical park, for instance), or law enforcement experience or training will have an edge.

Volunteering time with the National Park Service is another way to gain experience, although volunteer work does not necessarily help you obtain paid employment in park positions. Still, the relevant experience you gain may give you an edge in getting either a seasonal or a full-time position. Volunteer work also provides good contacts. At the very least, volunteer work with the National Park Service may provide a satisfying sideline for people otherwise employed.

Seasonal Firefighting

Each summer the forest service hires a number of seasonal employees to assist with fighting forest fires. Most of these jobs are in the western states of Alaska, California, Montana, Oregon, and Utah. Work for these firefighters, often known as smoke jumpers, is intense, and extensive training is necessary. New smoke jumpers usually receive about four weeks of training, and experienced jumpers generally get a week of refresher training. These positions require some previous firefighting experience and a season of general forest experience. Many people apply for these positions, but few are selected; previous firefighting experience, rigid physical conditioning, and excellent health are all required.

Summer workers are usually selected quite early (often in December of the previous year), so it pays to apply early. Applications can be made through the forest service or at state employment offices.

RESOURCES

General

The Canadian Nature Federation
Suite 606—1 Nicholas Street
Ottawa, Ontario K1N 7B7
Telephone: 1-800-267-4088 or 613-562-3447
Fax: 613-562-3371
Web: http://www.cnf.ca/index.html

Park Management

National Recreation and Park Association
22377 Belmont Ridge Road
Ashburn, VA 20148
Telephone: 703-858-0784
Fax: 703-858-0794
Web: http://www.nrpa.org

The National Park System

U.S. Department of the Interior
National Park Service
1849 C Street, NW
Washington, DC 20240
Web: http://www.nps.gov/pub_aff/jobs.htm

National Park Service Regional Offices:
Alaska Regional Office
National Park Service
2525 Gambell Street, Room 107
Anchorage, AK 99503
Telephone: 907-257-2574

Northeast Regional Office
National Park Service
U.S. Custom House
200 Chestnut Street, Room 322
Philadelphia, PA 19106
Telephone: 215-597-4971

Midwest Regional Office
National Park Service
1709 Jackson Street
Omaha, NE 68102
Telephone: 402-221-3456

National Capital Regional Office
National Park Service
1100 Ohio Drive, SW
Washington, DC 20242
Telephone: 202-619-7256

Intermountain Regional Office
National Park Service
12795 Alameda Parkway
Denver, CO 80225
Telephone: 303-969-2020

Southeast Regional Office
National Park Service
75 Spring Street Southwest, Suite 1130
Atlanta, GA 30303
Telephone: 404-331-5711

Pacific West Regional Office
National Park Service
600 Harrison Street, Suite 600
San Francisco, CA 94101
Telephone: 415-744-3888

Interpretation

>The National Association for Interpretation
>P.O. Box 2246
>Fort Collins, CO 80522
>Telephone: 970-484-8283; 888-900-8283
>Web: http://www.interpnet.com

Fish and Wildlife Management

>International Association of Fish and Wildlife Agencies
>444 North Capitol Street, NW, Suite 544
>Washington, DC 20001
>Telephone: 202-724-7890
>Fax: 202-624-7891
>Web: http://www.teaming.com/iafwa.htm

>U.S. Department of the Interior
>Fish and Wildlife Service
>Personnel Office
>Washington, DC 20240
>Web: http://www.fws.gov

>Canadian Wildlife Service
>Environment Canada
>351 St. Joseph Boulevard
>Hull, Quebec K1A 0H3
>Telephone: 819-997-1095
>Fax: 819-997-2756
>Web: http://www.cws-scf.ec.gc.ca/focus.html

Forestry

>Forest Service
>U.S. Department of Agriculture
>P.O. Box 96090
>Washington, DC 20013
>Web: http://www.fs.fed.us/people/employ/

Canadian Forest Service
Natural Resources Canada
580 Booth Street, Eighth Floor
Ottawa, Ontario K1A 0E4
Telephone: 613-947-7341
Fax: 613-947-7397
Web: http://www.nrcan.gc.ca/cfs/cfs_e.html

American Forests
P.O. Box 2000
Washington, DC 20013
Telephone: 202-955-4500
Fax: 202-667-7751
Web: http://www.amfor.org

Society of American Foresters
5400 Grosvenor Lane
Bethesda, MD 20814
Telephone: 301-897-8720
Fax: 301-897-3690
Web: http://www.safnet.org

National Recreation and Park Association
22377 Belmont Ridge Road
Ashburn, VA 20148
Telephone: 703-858-0784
Fax: 703-671-6772
Web: http://www.nrpa.org/

Conservation Districts

Obtain local addresses from:

National Association of Conservation Districts
9150 West Jewell Avenue, Suite 111
Lakewood, CO 80232
Telephone: 303-988-1892 or 1-800-825-5547
Fax: 303-988-1896
Web: http://www.nacdnet.org

Arboriculture/Horticulture
> Society of Municipal Arborists
> 7000 Olive Boulevard
> University City, MO 63130-2300
> Telephone: 314-862-1711
> Fax: 314-862-1711-329
> Web: http://www.urban-forestry.com

> The Golf Course Superintendents Association of America
> 1421 Research Park Drive
> Lawrence, KS 66049-3859
> Telephone: 1-800-472-7878
> Web: http://www.gcsaa.org

Landscape Architecture
> American Society of Landscape Architects
> 4401 Connecticut Avenue, NW
> Washington, DC 20008-3736
> Telephone: 202-898-2444
> Fax: 202-898-1185
> Web: http://www.asla.org/

Park or Wilderness Volunteer Positions
> American Hiking Society
> 1422 Fenwick Lane
> Silver Spring, MD 20910
> Telephone: 301-565-6704
> National Park Service
> Volunteers in Parks Coordinator
> P.O. Box 37127
> Washington, DC 20013-7127

> Bureau of Land Management
> Environmental Education and Volunteer Program
> 1849 C Street, NW, Suite LS-1275
> Washington, DC 20240
> Telephone: 202-452-5078

Seasonal Park and Firefighting Work

Forest Service
U.S. Department of Agriculture
Auditors Building
201 14th Street, SW at Independence Avenue, SW
Washington, DC 20024
Telephone: 202-205-8333
Fax: 202-205-1610
Web: http://www.fs.fed.us/

Seasonal Employment Program
Human Resources Office
National Park Service
P.O. Box 37127
Mail Stop 2225
Washington, DC 20013-7127
Telephone: 202-208-5074
Web: http://www.nps.gov/personnel/seasonal.html

Web Sites

Park Rangers on the Web—unofficial Web site for National Park Service rangers that describes the career of park ranger. (http://www.geocities.com/Yosemite/6081/)

Cool Works—a big clearinghouse of information about park careers that includes seasonal employment and has many links. (http://www.coolworks.com/showme/)

Cyber-Sierra's Natural Resources Job Search—links to environmental organizations, including information on summer jobs. (http://www.cyber-sierra.com/nrjobs/index.html)

Job listings for the U.S. government that include forestry and seasonal jobs: (http://www.usajobs.opm.gov/a.htm)

Profile

PARK RANGER RESOURCE MANAGER
Hank Snyder

"I always liked the outdoors and thought working in parks would be a good job," says Hank Snyder. Over the years he has worked in two state parks in California, for the U.S. Bureau of Land Management, and in six different national parks. He is currently a national park ranger at the George Washington Memorial Parkway in the Virginia suburbs of Washington, D.C. This parkway, developed as a memorial to George Washington, maintains the natural scenery of the Potomac River in a highly urban setting and leads to Washington's home, Mount Vernon, south of the Capitol.

Snyder began his park career in a maintenance job picking up trash on a beach and moved up in successive positions to his current post as a ranger resource manager. This progression through the ranks is fairly typical for park rangers.

"I spend 50 percent of my time outdoors and 50 percent indoors," explains Snyder. "Most people in these positions wish that they were outdoors more, but I like this mix. I have, however, turned down desk jobs." He admits that the pay is not high and adds wryly, "Park rangers have the saying that we 'get paid in sunsets.'"

Snyder has a bachelor's degree in geology and a master's in earth sciences. Although he doesn't use the coursework in his position, he certainly uses the skills that helped him get the degrees: writing, communications, and research. "The case reports, interpretive programs, and letters require good writing skills. Speaking is essential, because we are almost an entertainment industry. We must be able to relate to people."

Snyder lists helpful personality attributes for park rangers as gregariousness, tolerance, and flexibility. "We must be gregarious because we are constantly relating to people and tolerant because we deal with many people who may ask very obvious questions. Flexibility is important because we deal with so many different situations and types of people. We cannot be highly structured and doctrinaire."

Because of the numbers of people retiring from park positions, Snyder anticipates that there should be some openings. He suggests that if you want to work in the park service, you should "get your foot in the door through seasonal jobs or volunteer work. Learn to know people and make yourself indispensable to someone."

After more than twenty years of park work (seventeen in the U.S. Park Service), Snyder says with satisfaction that there is nothing about his job that he dislikes.

See Park Resource Management, page 53.

Profile

INTERPRETIVE NATURALIST
Roy Geiger

"Typically you don't get into interpretation unless you have a natural gift for gab and communication," says Roy Geiger, leaning back in the chair in his compact office. Coordinator of the education center and volunteer programs at the National Wildlife Federation's Laurel Ridge Center in Vienna, Virginia, since 1985, Geiger exemplifies the type of person he describes.

"Interpretive naturalists must be 'people persons' who can survive constant interruptions," Geiger adds. "Our principal job is to understand the jargon of the scientists and resource people and distill their information into language that the public understands."

After obtaining a bachelor of science degree in biology with an emphasis in wildlife, Geiger took a seasonal job as an environmental interpretive technician with the Bureau of Parks in Pennsylvania. He found a full-time position with a consulting firm working on contract with the Environmental Protection Agency. This job used his wildlife biology background, but Geiger declares that "living and working in a cubicle and pushing paper got old real fast." So he began working with the Wildlife Federation, initially as a laborer. "Because of my background as an interpretive naturalist, the job title quickly changed to *assistant naturalist*," says Geiger—and so did his job.

Geiger's expert knowledge of raptors, or birds of prey, made him a natural choice for a special tour throughout the United States with a live bald eagle. This national educational tour focused on bald eagles and other endangered species.

Geiger is responsible for all the educational activities at the Laurel Ridge Center—a blend of traditional nature center operations, visitors' center, and conference center that accommodates approximately thirty-nine thousand visitors annually. Geiger had a staff of three until budget cuts left him with one staff person and a very active corps of about seventy volunteers, who help maintain the program.

According to Geiger, "Most naturalists don't stay on the front lines of interpretation for a long time. To survive and make a decent salary, they work into management." In his management position, Geiger spends very little time working outdoors, which had been an initial attraction to this career. He now trains the teacher-naturalist volunteers to do the field naturalist work. "I've moved more into the role of supervisory mentor," he says.

"We see an increase of public interest in environmental concerns," he points out, "so I think there will continue to be a need for naturalists." Nevertheless, he advises those who are just entering the field to consider work with environmental consulting firms or as volunteers to maintain skills and make contacts while they look for a naturalist position.

Geiger likes being an educator and interpreting nature, the environment, and conservation issues to the public—"seeing the lightbulbs go on," as he puts it. "I also thoroughly enjoy the personal and professional contacts that I have in this field. I can call people across the country for advice in developing new programs.

"Probably the major thing that I dislike about the position is the bureaucracy," he concludes. "It can be very difficult." Geiger says that many interpretive naturalists are free spirits who find it onerous to have to "dot all the i's, cross the t's, and put everything into the proper proposal form. But it is possible," he adds with a twinkle in his eyes, "to turn the bureaucracy into a game and see how you can beat it or make it work for you."

See Interpretation, page 54.

Profile

FISHERIES BIOLOGIST
Bill Bradshaw

One typical position in fish and wildlife management is that of the fisheries biologist. "Biologists often plan, conduct, and report on studies about fish and fish habitat," says Bill Bradshaw, fisheries biologist with the Fish Division of the Wyoming State Game and Fish Department. "They also get involved in developing regulations, coordinating activities with other agencies or public groups, fisheries resource protection activities, and fish stocking."

Bradshaw works in the field from April through the summer collecting technical information. "I work with the in-stream flow crew, which determines the amount of water needed to maintain or improve a fishery system," he explains. "When I'm out collecting data, I may drive all day to get to a remote location because my job is statewide and I go all over the state. There I will collect hydraulic information for perhaps three or four days. In the winter, when I work in the office, I use this information to develop reports. It may take years to work out one project, especially if there are political considerations, such as negotiations with different government departments or agencies."

Bradshaw became a fisheries biologist by both "design and default." His original intention was to work in aquaculture (growing fish for market production), and he got a bachelor's degree in that field. "After an internship for the Washington State Department of Fisheries and several jobs, I decided to return to school for a master of science in fisheries instead of marine biology or aquaculture."

Specialized information required for his job includes knowledge of ecology, fish habitat needs, and hydraulics, especially stream hydraulics. Bradshaw adds, "Familiarity with computer models is also important. Some of these special skills I learned on the job—for example, the computer model.

"Writing and verbal communications skills are essential, because we spend a lot of time writing reports, as well as dealing with coworkers, state agencies, and the public."

Curiosity and the ability to get along with people are two important personality traits for this career. "I spend a lot of time camping out or in hotels with other people," says Bradshaw. "If you don't get along with the person you are working with, even though you may like the setting, the job can be drudgery. We also deal with the public and with persons in other state agencies. Curiosity is important because, as a trained scientist, I work at solving problems. Persons who get into management positions must be continually asking questions. This is a constantly evolving type of position."

Bradshaw believes the outlook for this type of work is good: "There are fairly many jobs, many of which are related to federal funding—usually a five-year allocation. The number will probably continue to grow."

If you're interested in this career, Bradshaw advises, "In looking for jobs, be persistent. Get temporary jobs even if this means that you move around. It's important to get experience and meet people. Employment experience is a different kind of educational experience. Keep an open mind and try to have a varied background. Flexibility in outlook and in the approach to solving problems is important."

The work does have a downside. Bradshaw cites as drawbacks the low pay and "the conservative political climate, which sometimes leads to disparaging or negative remarks about being a state employee." Further, he admits that "all of the travel in the summertime does get old." But he sums it up this way: "Overall, I like my job much more than I dislike it."

See Fish and Wildlife Management, page 55.

Profile

FOREST SUPERVISOR
Wendy Herrett

How did a landscape architect get to be a forester? "I got here by an unusual route," admits Wendy Herrett, forest supervisor for the Siuslaw National Forest in Corvallis, Oregon. "But landscape architecture is one of the paths to an administrative position in the U.S. Forest Service."

Herrett says she became interested in landscape architecture because "mountains and the outdoors have always been very attractive to me and I love to garden. Landscape architecture meshed my love of plants and the outdoors with design."

After completing a five-year bachelor's program in landscape architecture, Herrett obtained a job with the U.S. Forest Service, and she has held a variety of positions with the forest service since then. As a landscape architect, she worked in the regional office in Portland and in two forests: Mount Hood in Oregon, and Routt in Colorado. Her work included designing campgrounds, reducing the visible impact of timber activities in the forests, and training employees to be sensitive to the visual qualities of the scenery.

After six years as a landscape architect, Herrett began her move into management as resource assistant in Black Hills National Park in South Dakota. She spent several years as district ranger at the White River National Forest in Colorado before she moved to the legislative affairs staff in the forest service's Washington, D.C., office. Her responsibilities there included tracking legislation, writing testimonies, preparing and accompanying witnesses to hearings, and assisting members of Congress in drafting bills. After leaving Washington, she spent four years as deputy forest supervisor at the Mount Hood National Forest before assuming her present position.

As the forest supervisor, Herrett is in charge of administering all activities authorized by Congress, including camping, fisheries enhancement, special projects, trail maintenance and construction, and law enforcement. Her planning and managing functions include coordinating with other agencies, involvement with the public, and seeing that funds are spent within congressional boundaries. She supervises approximately 520 employees, five districts, and a Job Corps center, which provides vocational and educational skills.

Herrett says a sense of humor is essential in her job. "You shouldn't take yourself too seriously. You must be able to respond positively to criticism. Integrity is also important. You should care about the people you are trying to serve and about the land you are trying to protect. Your job is to mesh the needs of people with the desire to protect the land."

As an administrator, she spends a lot of time in meetings. "When I am in the field now, I deal mostly with employees rather than with projects," she explains. "I deal with personnel, disciplinary problems, hiring, resource issues, and decisions. It can be stressful, especially now, when more emphasis is placed on fewer resources. The job used to be simpler." She adds, regretfully, "I have worked less outdoors as I have moved up to higher positions."

Nevertheless, she likes her career. "It is rewarding when you come to a mutually acceptable solution of a controversy with a group of people," she says. "I like seeing the public enjoy their experience on the land and with the employees. It is fun to see the land. What I don't like is controversy; people can be nasty."

Herrett enjoys working with the forest service "because it exposes you to different points of view from both coworkers and the public. To work here one must be open to change and able to listen to more than one point of view. Solutions must be found where possible."

The ability to work with people is essential in forest management, which, Herrett points out, is not strictly a science. "It is important to be in touch with our feelings. Our publics express values based on their feelings, and we need to be able to relate to them and truly understand them so we can honestly consider what they are telling us when we make decisions.

"The career is cyclical and very competitive. With less land available now, timber jobs are not increasing. Jobs for foresters seemed to be on a downward trend for a while. Where there *is* an increase is in recreation and in wildlife and fish biology."

Herrett has this suggestion for those interested in this career: "Make sure you like working with people. Remember you are dealing with feelings and value systems, not facts. Be as flexible as possible in where you go and what you try, especially to get hired initially."

See Forestry, page 57.

Profile

CERTIFIED LANDSCAPE ARCHITECT
Wade Weaver

"I love the activity. There are times when the work is constant and I put in sixty-hour weeks. There is a lot of variety. I've worked with numerous forms of construction, from highways and industrial projects to residential sites, regional malls, shopping centers, and large office parks to a mine reclamation project." Wade Weaver's enthusiasm for his work in landscape architecture is apparent.

"I don't think there's anything that I really dislike about my job," he says candidly. Weaver, who works in Fairfax, Virginia, does admit that dealing with personal preferences and personality differences between professionals can be a challenge, but he adds quickly that this is found in every field.

Because a project's finished appearance is a good promotional tool, landscape architects are often involved in the early planning stages. Many times, however, the basic project is essentially laid out before the landscape architect is called in. At that point, according to Weaver, "You look at what is developed on the base sheets and formulate what the client and the architect are looking for and what should be done considering the various jurisdictions involved. Local zoning and state laws such as the canopy law [areas of the site that must be shaded by trees] must be taken into consideration."

Weaver indicates that the work can be very involved. "Rules and regulations are a hodgepodge of numerous directives. These are established by each county or region and have become very technical in the last few years." After graduation and required years of work in the field, landscape architects take a certification or licensure examination in the state where they work. Weaver is certified as a landscape architect in the state of Virginia.

The actual work of the landscape architect—the finishing touches—comes at the end of a project. The landscape architect must then take into account construction problems and a budget that may have been reappropriated. "At that point, with less money than earlier anticipated, the architect may have to review the plans drawn up before the project was begun," Weaver explains.

Weaver spent a total of seven years in preparation for his career. He initially spent two years each in civil and architectural engineering. Then he picked up additional credits in parks and recreation and in fine arts while completing a four-year landscape architecture degree program in three years.

Weaver readily admits that much of his work goes beyond the scope of traditional landscape architects because of his well-rounded education. "My education has been an asset in my current projects, and it has carried me in a recession. I've outlasted people who had more seniority. I'm still here on a workforce that, because of the economy, once shrank from 140 to 20 people." Weaver suggests that to weather economic downturns, a landscape architect should have a varied background; this will also provide more flexibility in job options.

His varied education and experience may also account for what Weaver calls his "forte in finding solutions to problems created by other landscape installation firms—for example, when the plant mix, while it presented a nice collage of colors and types, didn't succeed because it wasn't adaptable to the soil and shade conditions and the moisture restraints." He adds, "Many people think that a landscape architect is a gardener, but the work goes beyond that."

He sees the potential for the field to expand, especially considering the current focus on the environment and environmental problems. "I'm heavily into environmental issues right now. The landscape architect can take man-made features such as those used in storm-water management and turn them into a more natural setting. The work can help to improve water quality, facilitating erosion-control measures, and assist in the preservation of vegetation while improving maintenance operations for the site. It can be beneficial for the environment and for the resale or further development of the project."

Weaver suggests that landscape architecture is a good career for those who have an interest in nature and the environment and are "productive, energetic persons." He adds, "I would say general experience—being around construction, plant material, and so on—gives you a more rounded approach to the work. The education is important and beneficial, but I think you have to have something more: a desire to help people and nature."

The chief personality traits Weaver feels are necessary for this career are flexibility and congeniality. These are important, he explains, "because you have to work with other professionals." Other important qualities Weaver cites include being somewhat aggressive and willing to promote what you think is best. Landscape architects need to listen to the client, understand the needs, and pull the different concepts together, meshing and blending them. Weaver notes that landscape architects should have a well-rounded background and know where to get specialized information when it is needed.

"You will also look at how the thing fits together and how you will dovetail all the different aspects. Then you must disguise many things, such as utilities. Much of your work is buried," Weaver admits, laughing. "Many times no one recognizes the work, but you're the first one to be blamed when something doesn't look good."

See Landscape Architecture, page 62.

Chapter 5

Environmental Sciences

*We travel together, passengers on a little spaceship dependent
on its vulnerable supplies of air and soil: all committed for our
safety to its security and peace, preserved from annihilation
only by the care, the work, and I will say the love we give our
fragile craft.*

Adlai Stevenson

The sciences that focus on our environment—the environmental sciences—provide some work opportunities in the outdoors. The major fields in this category are geography, geology, meteorology, and oceanography. Each of these fields contains subspecialties.

Environmental scientists study the history, makeup, and characteristics of the atmosphere, surface, and core of the earth. Generally they study nonliving things, although there are some notable exceptions to this rule. Geographers, for example, study people and how they relate to their environment. Research is very important in these fields, as is the ability to apply the information gained in a practical manner.

GEOGRAPHY

Salary Range	Beginning salary around $20,000 to $25,000, average salary around $33,000, with the top end around $56,000
Educational Requirements	Minimum of a bachelor's degree; graduate study is an asset; master's needed for teaching in two-year colleges; doctorate needed for top government and

Employment Outlook   private-industry positions and teaching
in universities
Above average

Geography is both a natural and a social science. That is, it studies people and their environment, and it helps draw connections between the cultural and physical worlds. Although the work of geographers is directly related to the outdoors, a great deal of it takes place indoors. Some fieldwork may take place in remote areas in minimal living conditions.

Some topics of concern to geographers are acid rain, nuclear war, hazardous waste, low-income housing, and the growth of world population. With better international communications and more interdependence among world nations, the geographer's expertise in analyzing global patterns should become more important.

The two essential questions that geographers ask as they study are *where* and *why:* Where are things situated, and why are they situated at that location? The first question calls for a descriptive answer, the second for an analytic response. Geographers have traditionally gathered data through field observation—from the ground, balloons, aircraft, and satellites. This data provided the basis for making maps, the basic tools geographers use in presenting information. But with the current explosion of technology, geographers are able to use new methodologies—such as computers—in collecting, analyzing, and presenting data.

Most geographers specialize in one of several branches of geography.

Regional geographers specialize in a particular region, such as a river basin, island, nation, or perhaps whole continent. They examine all aspects of the area—physical, economic, political, and cultural—and may be contacted for assistance with regional problems.

Economic geographers follow economic activities of a region and document the use of regional resources, including communications, mining, farming, marketing, trade, and manufacturing.

Political geographers study how the natural resources and physical features of a specific political unit relate to politics on local, state, national, and international levels.

Urban geographers focus on urban problems that relate to geography and may help in planning new urban and suburban developments, such as residential areas, shopping centers, traffic-control systems, parking areas, plant locations, and other issues relating to the geography of a city.

Medical geographers study the effects of the physical setting on health, including pollution of air, soil, and water.

Physical geographers study the processes that create landforms, vegetation, oceans, and weather and the significance of these processes to humans. In a subspecialty, a *climatologic geographer* analyzes changing climatic patterns and reasons for the changes.

Cartographers research, design, and draw maps. A relatively new but rapidly growing subfield, Geographic Information Systems (GIS), uses computer graphics, artificial intelligence, high-speed communications, and satellite data to make maps. This is helpful for such things as forecasting worldwide weather, managing emergencies, and preventing crime.

As a discipline, geography provides students with a body of theory and methodologies leading to an analytic technique that can be used for various occupations. Almost one-quarter of all professional geographers today are employed in government at the federal, state, and local levels and in federal agencies, the armed forces, and international organizations. Few are employed under the actual job title of *geographer,* although many positions fall into this category, including cartographer, geographic analyst, map curator, land officer, international economist, intelligence officer, and soil conservationist.

Other geographers work in private business, which is increasingly using their skills. These positions involve industrial location analysis, market research, and transportation design and planning. Regional and metropolitan planning is another field for geographers that is developing quite rapidly. Publishers of maps, atlases, textbooks, encyclopedias, and news and travel magazines often employ geographers as writers and editors. Geographers also teach in universities and colleges.

GEOLOGY

Salary Range	Starting at around $21,000, averaging about $33,600, topping off at about $58,000
Educational Requirements	Those with just a bachelor's degree will face stiff competition; for research, an advanced degree is required; for teaching in a four-year college, a doctorate is required
Employment Outlook	Average

Geologists study the earth's crust by looking at the structure, history, and composition of the upper layers and at the physical processes that change the earth. Geologists may use their knowledge to explore the earth in search of groundwater, minerals, oil, and other natural resources. Increasingly, they have begun to play a role in cleaning up the environment. There are many different, often interrelated, disciplines in geology, and geologists often specialize in one of these.

Economic geologists help locate and develop natural resources such as minerals and fossil fuels. *Engineering geologists* study sites for the construction of airfields, bridges, buildings, dams, highways, tunnels, and other structures and work out geological engineering problems. *Environmental geologists* focus on pollution, urban development, land use, and resource development problems. *Geochemists* study the type and location of chemical elements in rocks and minerals. *Geochronologists* determine the age of rocks by calculating the rate at which certain radioactive elements decay. *Glaciologists* study the types, movement, causes, and effects of glaciers.

Hydrologists and *hydrogeologists* focus on surface and underground water supplies. *Marine geologists* study the ocean and the continental shelf. *Mineralogists* study and classify the origins, composition, and properties of minerals. *Mining geologists* work in tandem with engineers to develop mines for the safe recovery of minerals. *Paleobotanists* and *paleontologists* identify, study, and classify fossils. *Petrologists* study the origins and composition of rocks. *Planetary geologists* examine the moon, planets, and solar system. *Sedimentologists* examine the characteristics, movement, and origins of sedimentary deposits. *Stratigraphers* study the mineral and fossil content as well as the thickness, shape, and distribution of layered rocks. *Structural geologists* investigate rock formations and layers and the forces producing or changing them. *Volcanologists* examine the geologic phenomena related to volcanic activity.

Jobs in geology are available with a variety of employers. Petroleum exploration is directly tied to the world demand for oil; because current supplies of oil appear to be insufficient to fulfill this demand, staff may be hired for future exploration needs. Petroleum exploration work in the future will be very challenging as it becomes more sophisticated and highly computerized. It will also take place in increasingly remote and difficult locations such as deep in the oceans and in arctic, desert, and jungle areas.

The mining industry is another area where geologists are employed. This industry experiences boom-and-bust cycles, and the competition for jobs is keen. If you decide to work in exploration or mining geology, make sure that you have a strong enough interest in these fields to carry you through the bust periods.

Exploration geologists work to discover mineral deposits, often overseas or in quite remote locations. Mining geologists work to turn a mineral deposit into profit. These jobs call for dedication and travel, flexibility in location and relocation, and the willingness to terminate favorite projects because of economic factors. If you aren't willing to make these concessions, consider other employers—such as academic, government, and research organizations—whose work emphasizes applying science to the study and understanding of ore deposits. The field experienced a boom in the early 1990s, mostly in gold mining and exploration in Nevada, but the future is not clear.

Other major employers of geologists are the federal, state, and local governments. In the federal government, the largest employer by far is the U.S. Geological Survey in the Department of the Interior. Other Interior Department bureaus hiring geoscientists are the Bureau of Land Management and Reclamation, the Bureau of Mines, and the Minerals Management Service.

Geoscientists are also hired by the Departments of Agriculture, Defense, Commerce, and Energy and the Environmental Protection Agency. Hydrologists may be in demand because of the major water problems faced in some parts of the United States and a number of other countries throughout the world. At the state level, state geological surveys have the largest number of positions. Other state and local agencies tend to have more geologist openings in the areas of environmental regulation.

Although some opportunities for academic jobs in the geological sciences do exist, this is not an area of major employment.

Consulting opportunities in the geoscience-related areas of water resources, hazardous waste management, and process engineering look very promising. The best background for consulting work is a major in hydrogeology, geochemistry, civil engineering, or sanitary engineering, or a well-rounded study of geology. In addition to technical knowledge, graduates should be aware of policy and institutional issues, which can be learned through business management, economics, law, and planning courses.

Consulting work is subject to change, and consultants need to follow the changing market. For example, in the middle 1980s there was a great demand for consultants in the construction of dams and nuclear power plants. The emphasis in the early 1990s was on water resources and hazardous waste disposal and control. It now appears that the best opportunities in the early twenty-first century for geologists with experience and advanced degrees will be in environmental consulting, hydrogeology, and engineering geology. These specialties are useful in the ongoing cleanup of contaminated sites, a major focus of the Environmental Protection Agency, and to help companies and government comply with complex environmental regulations. To adapt to changing market needs, flexibility and a variety of skills are crucial in the consulting business. Continuing education and the ability to change focus are also essential.

See Profile, page 89.

METEOROLOGY

Salary Range	Depends on education and the employer; begins at about $18,700, with $50,500 as an average, and a high end of $100,000-plus
Educational Requirements	A bachelor's degree is the minimum for federal jobs, and a master's or doctorate is needed for teaching and research
Employment Outlook	Average or slower than average; jobs are more likely for people with advanced degrees and with the National Weather Service

The science of meteorology is concerned with observing, describing, understanding, forecasting, and possibly controlling the behavior of the atmosphere. Many of the basic meteorological instruments were developed centuries ago, when Galileo invented the thermometer in 1593 and Torricelli the barometer in 1643. Recent advances in the accuracy of measuring and observing weather conditions, faster communications, and use of satellites and computers in analyzing data have all contributed to an increased understanding of the atmosphere.

The best-known meteorologist in a community is the person who conveys weather forecasts to a local area—usually known as the weather forecaster. Meteorology careers, however, are not limited to weather forecasting, and media meteorologists make up only a very small percentage of individuals in the field. Indeed, only about one out of every eight meteorologists works in media.

Meteorological research is conducted in an effort to gain more understanding of the atmosphere. To do this, mathematical models, computers, and more recent technology such as Doppler radars and satellites are used. A major goal is improving skills in predicting weather-pattern changes to improve the quality of forecasting. Applied research goes a step farther—using the findings of basic research for specific functions such as designing aircraft, conserving water resources, controlling air pollution, and improving forecasting.

Meteorology also influences planning and design in engineering. Products must be able to withstand the ravages of the weather in the local environment. Whether bridges, highways, or buildings are being constructed, information on the atmosphere is an important factor to consider.

Weather forecasters play a major role in the economy of the country. Their information influences decisions about crop planting and harvesting, air transportation, and protection from weather hazards and pollution, among other things. Decisions made by the general public regarding travel and vacation plans are also affected. Some specialized areas are flood and hurricane forecasting, and forecasting to help local highway system personnel determine when to salt or plow roads.

The major employer of meteorologists nationally is the U.S. government. Private industry, especially consulting and research firms, also uses meteorologists. Consulting meteorologists help companies solve such problems as determining smokestack height or how to deal with solar exposure.

Another career possibility is teaching. Meteorology—or atmospheric sciences, as it is sometimes called—is now taught at many universities and colleges throughout the country. Meteorology teaching jobs are more plentiful in the environmental sciences, an important area of study today. Universities also provide research positions in meteorology.

A bachelor's degree in meteorology is the minimum education necessary for meteorology jobs. Those wanting to get into research will need more education. Meteorology can also be combined with another discipline (agriculture; astronomy; or civil, environmental, or electrical engineering) to provide an interdisciplinary career.

See Profile, page 91.

OCEANOGRAPHY

Salary Range	Beginning at about $18,500, averaging about $35,000, and topping off at about $85,000
Educational Requirements	Minimum of a bachelor's degree; graduate training gives the best advancement potential, and a doctorate is

required for many research positions
and college teaching
Employment Outlook   Average to slower than average

The oceanographer uses the basic sciences to study the oceans and the ocean environment. Oceanography is an interdisciplinary science that examines the biological, physical, chemical, and geological processes of the ocean. The *biological oceanographer* studies all types of marine life, from microscopic creatures up to the blue whale, the largest ocean mammal. The *chemical oceanographer* looks at the chemical composition and chemical reactions of the ocean's water. The *geological oceanographer* is concerned with mineral deposits on the seafloor and tectonic forces that influence ocean basins. And the *physical oceanographer* examines the motions of the seas— the currents, tides, and waves—and the density, salinity, and temperature of the water.

Oceanographers share a commitment to research and to put to good use the results of research projects. Some oceanographers go out to sea on research vessels to collect data, while others employ data from satellites or use computer modeling. In the future, oceanographers may live and work on the ocean floor; already experimental researchers have lived at depths of greater than two hundred feet.

The government is a major employer, employing about half of all oceanographers in the United States. Private industries, consulting firms, and educational institutions also have positions for oceanographers. The academic setting involves both teaching and research. Increasingly, industrial firms that manufacture oceanographic instruments and equipment or build ships are hiring oceanographers.

RESOURCES

Geography

Association of American Geographers
1710 Sixteenth Street, NW
Washington, DC 20009-3198
Telephone: 202-234-1450
Fax: 202-234-2744
Web: http://www.aag.org

Geology

American Geological Institute
4220 King Street
Alexandria, VA 22302-1502
Telephone: 703-379-2480
Fax: 703-379-7563
Web: http://www.agiweb.org

The Geological Association of Canada
Department of Earth Sciences
Alexander Murray Building, Room ER4063
Memorial University of Newfoundland
St. John's, Newfoundland A1B 3X5
Telephone: 709-737-7660
Fax: 709-737-2532
Web: http://www.esd.mun.ca/~gac

The Geological Society of America
3300 Penrose Place
P.O. Box 9140
Boulder, CO 80301
Telephone: 303-447-2020
Fax: 303-447-1133
Web: http://www.geosociety.org

American Association of Petroleum Geologists
P.O. Box 979
Tulsa, OK 74101-0979
Telephone: 918-584-2555
Fax: 918-560-2636
Web: http://www.aapg.org

Meteorology

American Meteorological Society
45 Beacon Street
Boston, MA 02108-3693
Telephone: 617-227-2425
Web: http://www.ametsoc.org/AMS/amshomepage.cfm

Canadian Meteorological and Oceanographic Society
112-150 Louis Pasteur
Ottawa, ON, K1N 6N5
Telephone: 613-990-0300
Fax: 613-993-4658
Web: http://www.meds-sdmm.dfo-
mpo.gc.ca/cmos/admin.html

Oceanography

American Geophysical Union
2000 Florida Avenue, NW
Washington, DC 20009
Telephone: 202-462-6900 or 1-800-966-2484
Fax: 202-328-0566
Web:http://www.agu.org

International Oceanographic Foundation
3979 Rickenbacker Causeway, Virginia Key
Miami, FL 33149
Telephone: 305-361-4888
Fax: 305-361-4711
Web: http://www.rsmas.miami.edu/iof/

Profile

GEOLOGIST
Norma Biggar

"Although geologists have the reputation of being loners, my job as a consultant is pretty communicative," says Norma Biggar with a smile. "It
involves a lot of teamwork."

As senior geologist and associate with a large consulting firm headquartered in Denver, Colorado, Biggar specializes in seismic hazards in
their Oakland, California, office. Located some sixty miles from the epicen-
ter of the 1989 Loma Prieta earthquake and a mile from the site of the dou-
ble-decker highway that collapsed during that quake, the firm is well
situated for dealing with earthquakes.

Biggar describes her job as a balancing act: "I conduct the technical
studies on some projects and manage others, review work by others in the

company, develop technical approaches for projects, develop budgets and write proposals, and occasionally give presentations to clients. No two days are ever alike."

To determine if there have been any major earthquakes in an area during the last ten thousand or so years, Biggar searches for landforms unique to faults along which earthquakes occur. To do this, she first examines published geologic maps and talks with other geologists who may have mapped faults in the area. Then she studies aerial photographs and may do aerial overflights from an altitude of about 3,000 feet for a firsthand view of ground features. Features of particular interest are then investigated on the ground. Each of these steps narrows the scope of the examination. "If a feature is suspected to be an active fault, we excavate one or more trenches—three feet wide and ten to fifteen feet deep—across it with a backhoe and log the fault features seen in the trench walls," she explains.

"The objectives are to define the fault zone and the style of faulting, and to learn when and how frequently the most recent earthquakes have occurred along the fault." Engineers use the data she gathers to deal with the perceived seismic risk when designing structures to withstand earthquakes.

Biggar chose to major in geology after enrolling in a geology class to complete college course requirements. "I found the course very interesting and the material very familiar. The fact that the prof was a woman may have had some influence on my interest," she adds candidly. "I like geology because it is a very interdisciplinary science and integrates biology, chemistry, physics, and rock mechanics into understanding the earth processes."

For the consulting work she does, Biggar says a master's degree or at least some graduate study is necessary. On-the-job experience is also important. Her own credentials include a bachelor's degree in earth science and a master's in geology. She joined her present company years ago on a summer job and never left.

Biggar says that an ability to think in three dimensions is important for geologists—they must visualize the earth's structures both within a hundred feet of the ground surface and to a depth of several miles. "We use multiple working hypotheses and visualize various scenarios; one needs to have an open mind in evaluating the situation and looking at it from many angles." Technical and report-writing abilities are also important, and a knowledge of computer applications is becoming more necessary.

Consultants need to be very flexible. "You must be able to deal with clients under tough time constraints who change their minds and want something else. You need to respond rapidly to change.

"I enjoy the novelty and the changeability of my work—and the opportunities to learn something about totally new areas," Biggar says. "Dealing with earthquakes also keeps me humble. I am frequently reminded of the insignificance of human activities when they are compared with the power unleashed in a large earthquake.

"I guess I dislike the same things I like," she adds with a chuckle. "It is difficult to create a realistic schedule several weeks or months in the future. While the flexibility requirements and travel can be challenging and fun, they are also disruptive to personal life. I have to help some of our clients, who aren't familiar with the complexities of the work, understand the amount of time it may take to obtain the product [report] they desire."

Biggar doesn't get outside as much now as she used to, but recently she spent two months outside on a field assignment and in a recent week she was out six days. "People on the staff level do most of the fun work," she says ruefully. "The amount of time outside and the quality of that outside time depend on the project."

Biggar says job availability for geologists will continue. Many nonpetroleum jobs are driven by regulatory compliance issues, which are becoming more pervasive in our society. The hot spots now for geologists are in hazardous waste. In fact, Biggar has recently transferred to the Las Vegas office to work on site characterization of a proposed high-level nuclear waste repository.

Biggar advises would-be geologists to get at least a bachelor's degree; to study a broad range of topics, including hydrology; and to develop investigative and writing skills through experience. She also recommends taking the geologic field trips available from different organizations to network and learn of local geologic issues and the work that others are doing. "Then I suggest finding someone who's enthusiastic about your field of interest and working with her," she adds.

See Geology, page 82.

Profile
METEOROLOGIST
Ken Rancourt

"Meteorology was a good major for me, because I like being outdoors and I like computers and mathematics," explains Ken Rancourt, staff meteorologist at the Mount Washington Observatory in New Hampshire.

A private, nonprofit research organization, the observatory is perched atop New Hampshire's highest mountain, Mount Washington, 6,288 feet above sea level. Rancourt points out that it is "strictly a weather observatory. We do not forecast the weather."

As part of the contract to provide accurate weather reports for the U.S. Weather Service, on-duty observatory staffers must take five to ten minutes every three hours to observe the weather, checking on such things as cloud cover and density. One of Rancourt's major functions is to handle the research that goes on at the station. Because Mount Washington experiences "the world's worst weather," it is a prime location for research on cold regions. The observatory contracts with various organizations, such as the U.S. Army, 3M, and the National Weather Service, to carry on research.

Staff members spend a week at a time on the mountain, from Wednesday to Wednesday. Two to three people are on duty at all times, working eight- to ten-hour shifts. When the new crew comes up with food and the mail, there is a shift meeting and then the off-duty shift leaves for the week.

A typical day begins at about 5:30 a.m. "The morning person gets the forecast from the weather service and an updated weather map and does the six o'clock observation," Rancourt details. "We do several taped radio broadcasts and a couple of live radio shows to disseminate the weather for the northern part of New Hampshire. On the live show, a five-minute broadcast, we talk about weather conditions at the summit and at the station at the base of the mountain; then we briefly discuss the weather map, what's happening in the general area, and the local forecast."

Rancourt says that because the main research goes on in the winter, the only reason to go outdoors in the summer is the weather observation every three hours. He adds, "You do get sort of cramped once in a while and go outside anyway. In the wintertime we may go out as frequently as once an hour. That means getting dressed in full weather regalia, taking measurements and pictures, or doing whatever is required by contract."

Because this is a relatively small observatory, with four basic staff members, everyone is required to do everything, Rancourt explains. "Both the museum manager and I do radio shows. He fixes the oil furnaces when they go out, and we all handle things such as propane problems. Many people do many things, and that's why the place works."

This brings Rancourt to a misconception he wants to correct. "I know a lot of people think that you must be lonely if you work on the summit of Mount Washington. We had twenty-one for supper on Saturday night. It's hard to be lonely when you're washing dishes for twenty-one people," he laughs, "especially since we let our guests help with the work. In the summer our crew swells to ten, with state park rangers and a night cleanup person."

Rancourt started college as an aerospace engineering major but "read the handwriting on the wall" when Boeing had its first big layoff in the late 1960s. He switched to meteorology after hands-on summer experience for the division of meteorology at Iowa University, which "really sparked my interest." Rancourt has both a bachelor's and a master's degree in meteorology.

Failing to find a meteorology job right after graduation, Rancourt worked for a construction company for a while, then moved to a company that supplied radar equipment to schools. In this job he combined knowledge of electronics and meteorology. He has been at Mount Washington for more than ten years, and finds his construction knowledge a plus because, given the difficulty of winter travel, it isn't always easy to get a carpenter or plumber, and the ability to fix things is important.

"On the job I'm more of a support person, even though I have degrees in meteorology," he says. "But it's important to have someone with my experience here so that we can help set up effective research."

It is essential for a meteorologist to be able to use computers and work with statistical analysis. Rancourt adds, "You have to be personable and like communicating with the general public. It is also important to be able to work with a team. And a background in the physical sciences is essential."

Rancourt does find the week-on, week-off schedule difficult, but confides, "I think I'm pretty lucky. I really do like my job, and that makes this schedule easier to handle."

He cautions that his job is not typical of many meteorological positions, but, he asserts, "One thing that is typical of all meteorologists is that we enjoy watching the world around us—clouds, as well as the life around us, the lichens, the mosses, and the animals. Most meteorologists are interested in the out-of-doors."

See Meteorology, page 85.

Chapter 6

Engineering

A problem well stated is a problem half solved.
Charles F. Kettering

The profession of engineering dates back to the earliest records in history. People who built irrigation canals, palaces, temples, roads, baths, aqueducts—any structures designed to meet the needs of others—were called engineers. In military preparation and campaigns, engineers built forts and machines of war.

Engineers work to find solutions to specific practical problems confronting society. They take abstract scientific principles and technical knowledge and translate these into practical applications in the process of designing solutions to problems.

As our society changes and the problems we confront change, the field of engineering has also been evolving. Additionally, new materials and processes are enabling engineers to use more advanced technologies, and the profession is growing in importance.

There are at least fifty engineering specialties, most of which stem from what are considered the "classical" branches of engineering. Because engineers work to solve problems, new subfields are constantly being developed as new types of problems emerge. The following are the fields generally considered as the classical branches of engineering.

Aeronautical engineers research, develop, design, and test vehicles—both manned and unmanned—that operate above or below the surface of the earth.

Agricultural engineers are concerned with developing, maintaining, and using farm equipment and buildings, as well as raising crops efficiently and taking care of the needs of farm animals.

Bioengineers apply the technology of other engineering fields to the health and comfort of human beings. This is the most recent addition to the classical branches.

Ceramic engineers work with developing and applying materials, either natural or synthetic, made from inorganic matter whose value results from high-temperature processing. Some of the products are pottery, lasers, semiconductors, and protective shields for space travel.

Chemical engineers design, develop, and apply the processes that change raw materials in their chemical construction and material shape. Some of the products of these processes are fuels, fertilizers, plastics, and paper.

Civil engineers are concerned with building the structures that relate to community life, such as houses, office and public buildings, shopping malls, highways, railroads, bridges, tunnels, and dams. This is the oldest classical engineering branch.

Electrical engineers work in electronics, power, and information processing. Computer engineering, which may soon be considered a separate branch, is still considered to be a part of electrical engineering. This is one of the largest engineering branches in terms of the number of practitioners.

Industrial engineers are involved with the cost and construction of goods. These engineers work mostly in plants, coordinating personnel, materials, and machinery and deciding the best way to use each of these to produce the most economical product.

Mechanical engineers are concerned chiefly with planning and operating the machines that produce and relay power.

Metallurgical engineers, unlike others, are more involved with matter than with machines, power, or structures.

AGRICULTURAL ENGINEERING

Salary Range	Starting at about $28,000 and averaging $62,000 to $75,000
Educational Requirements	College
Employment Outlook	Good

Career opportunities in agricultural engineering vary widely both in type of work and in location. Agricultural engineers are involved in all facets of food production, processing, marketing, and distribution. They take ideas and concepts and use mathematical, biological, and physical principles to make these ideas become reality. And their work may take them to countries all around the globe.

There are four main areas in agricultural engineering: *product design* mainly involves designing specific products such as machinery or structures; *systems engineering*, which includes irrigation equipment and environmental, electrical, microprocessor-control, and farmstead types of engineering; *resource engineering*, which involves water quality and management; and *process engineering*, which pertains to food and crop processing and crop production.

The agricultural engineering graduate may be involved in developing machines to make work easier; controlling pollution; preserving and protecting dwindling land, air, and water resources; developing new food products; and increasing food productivity. Other possibilities in this subfield include work in quality control, consulting, and sales and management.

Job locations for agricultural engineers vary considerably; they may be in rural areas or in major population centers. Many agricultural engineers work overseas helping developing countries increase agricultural production or assisting with soil and water conservation.

With the increase in world population and the concomitant demand for more food, job opportunities for agricultural engineers are increasing. For example, agricultural engineers are currently finding more work in the machinery area.

The following industries are among those that hire agricultural engineers: biosystems, including bioprocessing and biotechnology for food and other industries; food processing, including handling grains and other crops, storing processed foods, and safety and quality issues around food processing; structures and environment, including facility design for housing and maintaining livestock; power and machinery, including developing, designing, testing, and selling equipment or systems; and environmental quality, including working for government agencies or consulting firms on issues of improving air, land, and water conservation and quality.

CIVIL ENGINEERING

Salary Range	Starting at about $28,600, averaging about $46,500, and topping off at around $89,000
Educational Requirements	College plus training
Employment Outlook	Very good

Civil engineers design and supervise construction of the physical infrastructures necessary for modern life. Among the historical responsibilities of the civil engineer were building bridges, highways, dams, aqueducts for conducting water, and canals. Tunnels, water-supply systems, pipelines, and irrigation and sewerage systems are also the concern of the civil engineer. More recently, civil engineers have been occupied in building airports and ballistic missile facilities, creating technology for space exploration, and controlling air and water pollution.

Civil engineers work at building structures that are strong and safe, and that conform to government regulations and building codes. They are involved in surveying the building site, preparing it for construction, and selecting the correct materials. Knowing how to use construction equipment—such as bulldozers, power shovels, and cranes—is essential.

This branch can be divided into six broad categories: construction, structural, transportation, hydraulic, foundation, and sanitary engineering. *Construction engineers* coordinate the designs of other engineers, prepare the land, schedule construction, and handle all field supervision. *Structural engineers* are concerned with analyzing forces and materials and how they interact; they design bridges, subways, large buildings, dams, and piers. *Transportation engineers* are concerned with traffic control and flow, as well as designing highways, railroads, waterways, and airports. *Hydraulic engineers* work with dams, reservoirs, canals, irrigation projects, and water-supply systems. *Foundation engineers* know how soils behave under stress and give data to the structural engineer to aid in preparing designs. *Sanitary engineers* design facilities to provide clean water, dispose of wastes, and control pollution. The term *civil engineer* initially meant "a builder of civil or domestic structures." Over the years, civil engineering has changed and adjusted as civilization has changed. This flexibility will likely continue, and some of the new specialties may gain in importance and become branches separate from civil engineering. Civil engineering offers a wide range of career choices. It's possible to combine any of the various subcategories or specialties into a career that is well suited to your own interests.

See Profile, page 107.

ENVIRONMENTAL ENGINEERING

Salary Range	Starting at about $23,000, averaging about $40,000, and topping off at about $75,000
Educational Requirements	College is the minimum requirement; a master's degree and doctorate give advantages in finding better jobs and in advancement
Employment Outlook	Excellent

Environmental engineering is an example of a profession evolving to fill recognized needs. It has only been recognized as a separate professional category in the last twenty-five years, although the work was performed for decades before that. The environmental engineer is involved in protecting the environment and controlling wastes. The major areas include air pollution control, hazardous waste management, industrial hygiene, public health, toxic materials control, radiation protection, storm-water management, land management, wastewater management, solid waste disposal, and water supply.

Environmental engineers can select from a great variety of employers and locations. Organizations employing environmental engineers include industries and private businesses; consulting engineering firms; research firms; government agencies at the federal, state, and local levels; testing laboratories; and universities. These employers and the sites on which the work is performed are located around the world.

Work for environmental engineers can be indoors or out. Typically, the mix will be 25 percent outdoors and 75 percent indoors. There are, however, many jobs where all of the work is done outdoors. Most environmental engineering positions are in locations with a high concentration of people, because that is where pollution problems generally occur. Types of jobs include researching, designing, planning, and operating pollution-control facilities; working for government regulatory agencies; managing programs; teaching; and working in professional societies.

The best preparation for an environmental engineering career is a degree in environmental, civil, mechanical, or chemical engineering. A master's degree or a doctorate will give you an edge; more employers now give preference to candidates with advanced degrees. The basic components of engineering degrees are math, science, and engineering mechanics courses. And because environmental engineering is involved with people, it is also important to know how individuals and societies function—you should also take humanities courses. Writing and speaking skills are important for engineers, and these should be a part of both formal studies and extracurricular activities. To solve problems, engineers have to communicate well with people, and communications skills can only be learned and perfected by using them.

Because jobs for environmental engineers outnumber candidates, this is a rather secure field to enter. The work is constantly changing as conditions, policies, and environmental challenges change. A commitment to lifelong learning is important, because environmental engineers will likely need to retrain several times in the course of their working careers.

See Profile, page 108.

GEOTECHNICAL ENGINEERING

Salary Range	Starting at about $28,600, averaging $47,000, and topping off at around $89,000
Educational Requirements	College plus training
Employment Outlook	Very good

Geotechnical engineering is a branch of civil engineering. These engineers design and construct structures that are underground, on the ground, or made out of the ground. Tunnels, pipelines, and underground openings are examples of structures constructed underground. Bridges, roadways, dams, wastewater treatment facilities, and landfills are all constructed on the ground. Works constructed out of the ground (soil and rock) include dams, canals, highway embankments, and landfills.

For construction on the ground, geotechnical engineers are involved at the beginning of the project. They test to determine soil conditions and movements, both by drilling to obtain samples of the soil and rocks on the site and by observing the geology. Based on their laboratory analysis of this information, they prepare reports recommending specifications for the kinds of materials that should be used for each particular type of facility. Monitoring the facility during construction to verify the accuracy of their testing is an essential part of geotechnical engineering.

Standard training for a geotechnical engineer is a bachelor's degree in civil engineering plus a master's in civil engineering with a geotechnical engineering specialty; few individuals practice geotechnical engineering without a master's degree. A doctorate qualifies you for a specialty within the field, such as earthquake engineering. Geotechnical engineering students take a heavy concentration of geology courses in addition to science and mathematics.

Waste management engineering, a part of geotechnical engineering, is a fast-growing subfield because of the tremendous problems that countries around the world are facing in solid waste management, hazardous waste, and toxic cleanup. Because they often deal with ground or groundwater contamination and landfill sites, geotechnical engineers will continue to provide assistance in solving those problems.

See Profile, page 110.

PETROLEUM ENGINEERING

Salary Range	Starting at about $42,600, averaging about $50,600, and topping off at around $87,000
Educational Requirements	College is the minimum requirement
Employment Outlook	Slower than average; will improve if the price of oil rises

The petroleum engineer develops and produces energy economically and safely from resources deep inside the earth, sometimes even under the sea; these include oil and natural gas, as well as geothermal resources. Because these resources can be studied only from the surface, which may be a mile above, the petroleum engineer has to use modern technologies and many sciences to learn about deposits and develop them.

Petroleum engineers may specialize in different areas. A *drilling engineer* chooses necessary equipment for a drilling rig, estimates the costs, and supervises the entire drilling process. A *production engineer* uses chemical or mechanical means to maximize production from oil and gas wells already in use. A *reservoir engineer* works to find the best method to develop a reservoir of natural energy; these methods may include injecting water, gas, or steam, or using chemical flooding to obtain the natural resources as economically as possible.

Petroleum engineers work indoors and outdoors in settings as different as research laboratories and offshore drilling rigs. They work at locations all around the world for large integrated oil companies or for firms that only explore and produce petroleum for others to refine and sell. Some positions for petroleum engineers are available with all levels of government. Universities have some teaching and research opportunities; petroleum engineers can also work as corporate consultants.

Demand for petroleum engineers is not constant; this industry is subject to many ups and downs. Because the need for energy will continue to be a factor of modern life, however, it is likely that there will continue to be openings in this area of engineering. If you're interested in becoming a petroleum engineer, you'd be wise to check the current and anticipated market for the field before investing too much time and money in study.

SURVEYING

Salary Range	Beginning at about $14,000, averaging about $28,000, and topping off at about $48,000
Educational Requirements	Bachelor's degree
Employment Outlook	Good, but slower growth than average

Surveying is one of the most relentless of outdoor jobs. All of the field surveys—which constitute more than half the work—are spent in the outdoors; an interest in working outdoors is thus essential for individuals in this occupation. Although the summer months are the prime working period, surveyors actually work year-round in all types of weather conditions.

Surveyors take exact measurements that determine property boundaries and provide the information needed to make maps, on construction projects, and for other engineering uses. In essence, the surveyor provides exact measurements for a particular geographic area, noting the elevations and contours on the earth's surface.

Any job for which precise measurements are needed will use surveyors—indeed, surveyors are the first workers to be involved in these jobs. One of the most common needs is for construction projects, such as superhighways, bridges, and housing developments. Surveyors usually work with several other individuals, such as surveying and mapping technicians and instrument assistants. These assistants support the surveyor, handle the surveying instruments, and record measurements.

Surveyors usually become expert in one or several of the different types of surveying. *Land surveyors* establish boundary lines for a specific region, property, or other land tract to help in preparing deeds. *Highway surveyors* are essential in planning new highways or highway additions. *Marine surveyors* measure the depth of harbors, rivers, and other bodies of water for navigation projects and for planning and building dams, bridges, breakwaters, and piers. *Mine surveyors* record both the surface and underground areas of a mining operation to help in design and evaluation as well as in assessing the type and amount of raw material available. *Geophysical prospecting surveyors* search for and mark areas that are likely to contain deposits of petroleum. *Pipeline surveyors* work to establish rights-of-way for oil pipeline construction, establishing property lines and collecting the information necessary to lay the lines.

Surveyors most likely to use highly technical equipment, including the latest computer and satellite measuring data or high-tech photographic equipment, are the geodetic surveyors and the photogrammetric engineers. The *geodetic surveyor* measures such a large area that the curvature of the earth must be taken into account. *Photogrammetric engineers* use photo surveying—photogrammetry—to determine the contour of an area, showing features such as mountains, lakes, rivers, forests, and other very specific landmarks. This technique is especially helpful in surveying areas that are inaccessible or contain difficult terrain.

Essential high school courses for surveying are algebra, geometry, trigonometry, physics, and mechanical drawing or a similar drafting course. Common college backgrounds are surveying or engineering—usually civil engineering with a surveying emphasis. To advance in the highly technical areas, graduate study is essential.

Surveyors must be able to work with other people, often in supervisory positions. Surveyors have to perform mathematical computations accurately and quickly, and they must be able to visualize and understand the spatial relationships of various objects, differentiating and comparing shapes, sizes, and other forms. Because surveyors do a lot of walking and often need to carry equipment through all types of terrain, they must be physically fit and coordinated. Surveyors also need to be licensed or registered with the state or province in which they work.

Although surveyors usually work a standard forty-hour week, overtime may be required to keep a project on schedule. The hazards of survey work, which depend mainly on the region and climate, include poisonous snakes, poison ivy, sunburn, and frostbite. Surveyors working near large construction projects or busy highways also run the risks of heavy traffic and accidents due to congestion.

Increasingly, as the technology improves, satellites are used to survey vast areas or large mountains. Work in remote areas is becoming infrequent, and additional training may be required to use this highly technical equipment. The work location for a surveyor is likely to change from survey to survey, and some assignments may require working away from home for a period of time.

SURVEYING TECHNOLOGY

Salary Range	Beginning at about $13,800, averaging about $27,000, and topping off at about $43,900
Educational Requirements	A high school diploma is the minimal educational requirement
Employment Outlook	Slower than average

A surveying technician is the leading assistant for a professional surveyor or civil engineer and is usually the first person involved in jobs that require precise measurements. These include the construction of highways, bridges, dams, mines, airports, housing developments, and all types of buildings. Surveying technicians may specialize in one particular type of surveying, especially if they join a firm that focuses on a specific type or types of surveying.

Most surveying technicians are employed in actual construction, where their services are required throughout a project to ensure that the structure adheres to engineering specifications—such as size, height, and depth—as work progresses. They follow design plans to locate critical construction points such as building corners or foundation detail points; always, they provide the precise measurements needed to keep construction projects on track and on specification.

Other survey technicians survey land to establish boundary lines for townships or properties; measure large masses of land, sea, or space for a geodetic surveyor; chart bodies of water for hydrographic surveyors; and establish points of reference for constructing highways, railways, and pipelines. Technicians who work for mining companies may survey the ore reserves or detail a map of existing mines; they may also help determine potential areas to explore as new mines.

To survey large or inaccessible areas, photogrammetry—special equipment in an airplane or a ground station—may be used. This aids in planning highways, preparing topographical maps, or measuring areas planted in a certain crop to verify government quotas. Using this highly technical equipment requires additional training.

While a high school diploma or equivalent is the basic requirement, additional education—such as that provided by a two-year technical school—is essential for advancing on the job. High school courses should include all of the math and science available as well as English, any communications courses, and any computer courses.

High school graduates may want to enter the field immediately after graduation, especially if the company offers on-the-job training. Because technical training is important to advance in this career, though, it may be better to obtain this training before entering the field. Many surveying technicians later get a bachelor's degree in engineering or surveying. After working for a certain length of time, some take an examination and become licensed as land surveyors. Currently, surveying technicians do not need to be licensed or registered.

Some of the requirements for surveying technician jobs include great interest in working outside; good physical conditioning, especially to get to remote areas and to carry around the surveying equipment; and physical coordination. Mathematical skills, especially quick and accurate calculations, are essential. Working as part of a team is necessary, and a good grasp of English grammar and spelling is also important for writing the reports and letters that are a part of a technician's work. It is essential to be able to visualize objects in two or three dimensions and to differentiate among and compare shapes, sizes, and aspects of objects.

Working outdoors as a surveying technician involves many hazards similar to those faced by the surveyor; these include climate (sunburn, heat exhaustion, frostbite) and local plants and animals (poisonous snakes, poison ivy). Survey projects in busy construction or urban areas also present problems of highway traffic and flying debris. Additionally, outdoor work locations usually change from project to project, and a technician may need to be away from home for a period of time.

RESOURCES

General

Society of Women Engineers
United Engineering Center
120 Wall Street, 11th Floor
New York, NY 10005
Telephone: 212-509-9577
Fax: 212-509-0224
Web: http://www.swe.org/

American Association of Engineering Societies
1111 19th Street, NW, Suite 403
Washington, DC 20036-3690
Telephone: 202-296-2237
Fax: 202-296-1151
Web: http://www.aaes.org

Canadian Council of Professional Engineers
116 Albert Street, Suite 401
Ottawa, Ontario K1P 5G3
Telephone: 613-232-2474
Fax: 613-230-5759
Web: http://www.ccpe.ca

Agricultural Engineering

The Society for Engineering in Agricultural, Food, and Biological Systems
2950 Niles Road
St. Joseph, MI 49085-9659
Telephone: 616-429-0300
Fax: 616-429-3852
Web: http://asae.org/

Civil Engineering

American Society of Civil Engineers
1801 Alexander Bell Drive
Reston, VA 20191-4400
Telephone: 703-295-6000 or 1-800-548-2723
Fax: 703-295-6222
Web: http://www.asce.org

Environmental Engineering

American Academy of Environmental Engineers
130 Holiday Court, Suite 100
Annapolis, MD 21401
Telephone: 410-266-3311
Fax: 410-266-7653
Web: http://www.enviro-engrs.org

Geological and Geophysical Engineering

Colorado School of Mines
Golden, CO 80401
Telephone: 303-273-3000
Web: http://gn.mines.colorado.edu:80/
Information is available from the geology and geological
engineering department and from the geophysics depart-
ment.

Petroleum Engineering

Society of Petroleum Engineers
Customer Service/Books Department
P.O. Box 833836
Richardson, TX 75083-3836
Web: http://www.spe.org/store/aids.html

American Institute of Mining, Metallurgical and Petroleum
Engineers
Three Park Avenue
New York, NY 10016-5998
Telephone: 212-419-7676
Fax: 212-271-9622
Web: http://www.idis.com/aime

Surveying

American Congress on Surveying and Mapping
5410 Grosvenor Lane, Suite 100
Bethesda, MD 20814-2144
Telephone: 301-493-0200
Fax: 301-493-8245
Web: http://www.acsm-hqtrs.org/acsm/

American Society for Photogrammetry and Remote Sensing
5410 Grosvenor Lane, Suite 210
Bethesda, MD 20814
Telephone: 301-493-0290
Fax: 301-493-0208
Web: http://www.asprs.org

Engineering Web Site
Society for Mining, Metallurgy, and Exploration:
(http://www.smenet.org/)

Profile

CIVIL ENGINEER
Dennis McDonough

"Everything is outdoors or outdoor-related activities." Regional engineering supervisor Dennis McDonough exudes enthusiasm as he talks about his job with the Ducks Unlimited (DU) regional office in Jackson, Mississippi. McDonough, who has a bachelor's degree in civil engineering, works as a regional biologist. "We do habitat enhancement," he explains. "We travel to a site in pairs: a biologist and an engineer. There the biologist determines the habitat needed and the engineer comes up with the concept and design to provide that habitat. It's a perfect job."

McDonough previously worked in the DU North Dakota office, where, he says, "We did all nesting or production habitats. This means work with dams, dikes, islands, level ditching, and that type of engineering. We did some fairly deep water impoundment to provide secure water for nesting." In Jackson, DU provides migratory habitats. Now, McDonough relates, "I work with shallow water covering a larger area, but the function is the same. The biologist still determines what is needed for a habitat, and the engineer comes up with the design structures."

McDonough details his experience: "I spent fourteen years with the U.S. Soil Conservation Service and four years with the forest service before I went to work with DU in 1985. With the Soil Conservation Service, the experience was technical—we built dams, dikes, levees, and irrigation. When I was with the forest service, I was mainly concerned with road building. After ten years as an engineering tech, I figured out that getting an engineering degree was the only way I'd be able to do what I really wanted to do. I was working in western North Dakota with the forest service in 1985 when DU started their new habitat office out there. They were staffing up, so I began as a technician with them before working into a regional biologist position."

It's a move he has not regretted. "The thing I like most about the switch is that I don't do anything that is destructive. Everything I do is very positive; I am always making something better, either enhancing or creating. I have not done a project with DU that has given me any remorse or regrets whatever about what I was doing to the environment. I feel fortunate about that, because I don't think a lot of engineers have that same opportunity. It's great!"

McDonough estimates that he spends 50 percent of his time outdoors and 50 percent indoors. "We're able to break it up fairly well, too," he adds. "It isn't like I'm in the office for a month and then out for a month. Several days a week really makes it a nice mix."

Although McDonough works mainly with the biologist on the team, he also teams up with state and federal managers. On occasion he even finds it necessary to address a group. "Public speaking ability is a very important attribute in my job. I also do a lot of letter and report writing. Proper paperwork to support our projects is necessary to obtain permits."

Unfortunately, jobs like this are few. McDonough offers some advice for those who find his job attractive. "The perfect engineer for wildlife in general would be a combination of civil and environmental. Combining the civil engineer's training in soils and foundations, which would allow him to build or create an outdoor habitat, with an environmental engineer's expertise in water treatment and water quality would give a new graduate an unlimited ability in working with wildlife.

"I wish there were a lot of job openings," he adds. "More habitats and resources are needed but funds are not available. You may need to take a job that you're not totally enamored with but that will give you good experience to add to your résumé for the time when you find the job you've always wanted. And you might start as a technician, as I did, and work into higher-level jobs as they become available."

See Civil Engineering, page 97.

Profile

ENVIRONMENTAL ENGINEER
Kathleen Schaefer

Kathleen Schaefer says that her choice of environmental engineering came by fluke, not by design. "When I went to college I decided to major in engineering on a whim," she explains. "Fortunately, my high school counselor hadn't let me drop math and science, so I had the technical background to get into engineering."

Schaefer initially took her bachelor's in civil engineering into a job in facilities engineering but changed to environmental engineering because there was more demand in that field. She is now working toward a master's degree in chemical engineering.

Schaefer is a water resources engineer with a Fairfax, Virginia, engineering consulting firm. "My basic concern is with clean water," she says. "If it is not clean I will see that it is cleaned after industrial use."

Use of the computer, especially for modeling water systems, is very important on Schaefer's job. "Computers have given us capabilities to solve problems that were too difficult to solve in the past when we followed rules of thumb and tables. With the computer we can model the specific water system, define the migration of pollutants much better, and make much closer calculations."

Schaefer likes the variety her job provides. Although each day is different, a sample day could begin by meeting with a client to discuss a problem with a water system. Then she would model the system on the computer, analyze the situation from the model, and write a report. She would also call the appropriate regulatory agency to confirm the pertinent regulations.

Although she doesn't get outside as much as she would like—"I now go out about two days a month, but it goes in spurts from a solid week out to three months without any outdoor work"—being outdoors is another aspect of environmental engineering that Schaefer really likes. She also enjoys client interaction. On the downside, she says that big, time-consuming projects begin to get old after a while.

Schaefer cites math and science as key background courses for environmental engineering. Enjoying the outdoors is also important. Computer knowledge is essential, but Schaefer says that the models and tools are changing rapidly and can be learned on each job. She advises learning a computer language and gaining basic familiarity with computers rather than intensive study.

Although Schaefer says career paths for environmental engineers are quite varied, a typical pattern begins with the engineer working on some aspect of design for seven to ten years and then becoming a project manager who supervises three to five engineers. The next step up is department manager, with supervisory responsibility for ten to thirty engineers. Becoming principal of a firm is the final step.

"One of the bad things about engineering," she confides candidly, "is that although engineers make more money initially than people in many other careers, the pay levels off rapidly."

One project she remembers with pleasure involved work on a site adjacent to Puget Sound in Seattle with a wood-treatment plant whose chemicals had seeped into the groundwater system. The client was willing to clean up the area but lacked money for the immediate massive cleanup mandated by the regulatory agencies. "This project took two engineers two years to work on," she remembers. "The situation was made more difficult because of the tide fluctuation, and I spent a lot of time in the field. We had a wonderful client for whom I had a lot of empathy.

"The ability to write is very important on my job," says Schaefer. "I write proposals and reports—guidance on doing the job and a summary of the work that has been done. The wording can be very important." Schaefer admits that she had to study on her own to improve her writing.

She also suggests that a broad background is especially helpful in this field. "I would encourage environmental engineers to take more liberal arts courses, because they need to understand sociology and philosophy as well as technical matters."

Schaefer cites no one specific personality trait that environmental engineers should have but points out that all engineers need to be inquisitive about how things work and enjoy solving problems. She adds, "The field is so diverse that you can find your own niche, no matter what it is."

See Environmental Engineering, page 98.

Profile
GEOTECHNICAL ENGINEER
Art O'Brien

"You have to like to get your hands dirty to be a geotechnical engineer," declares Art O'Brien, "because when you're out gathering samples you will get dirty. And you're out in all kinds of weather and all seasons."

Hands-on work was not the only thing that attracted Art O'Brien to his career. "My enjoyment of the outdoors was a part of the reason for choosing geotechnical engineering," this soft-spoken engineer admits quickly. "Initially I went into civil engineering to use my math and science interests. Geotechnical engineering, a branch of civil engineering, interested me because there's a lot of judgment involved. I also liked the fact that we take projects from the very beginning to the very end."

O'Brien has a bachelor's degree in civil engineering and a master's in civil engineering with a geotechnical engineering specialty. He is currently the department manager for the Solid Waste Engineering Group at an engineering firm in Hernden, Virginia. His fondness for geotechnical engineering is evident as he speaks about the career.

Some of the skills needed for this career aren't necessarily learned in school, O'Brien points out. "Writing can be learned on the job or in writing courses after graduation. People management skills are also needed. Encouraging and motivating people—not only peers and people working in the company, but also subcontractors outside the company—are important.

"One of the difficult things about geotechnical engineering," he admits, "is that the natural materials you're dealing with—properties deposited by Mother Nature—are often highly variable. Oftentimes your testing isn't necessarily representative, so you have to be alert for changes. That can be frustrating." Major changes don't often need to be made, he adds, but small changes requiring quick adjustments do. "But if you're out there you can usually make those changes quickly and they don't affect the progress of the project."

O'Brien indicates that new graduates with master's degrees usually start out as staff engineers. "They do field observations. As the career progresses, less time is spent outside and more time managing and planning. The next level is project engineer, and then project manager. The project management role means more time spent as a team leader working with the client and guiding and managing the project and staff engineers, who are gathering information and doing analyses. A next step may be starting your own business."

About his current management position, O'Brien says, "I have taken my geotechnical engineering experience and related it to the solid waste side of geotechnical engineering. So I've expanded my geotechnical engineering into a much broader perspective.

"That means," he adds regretfully, "that I don't get out as much as I used to." He's not sorry he made this move, however. "In my current position I have to keep lots of balls in the air and don't have the opportunity to focus on one specific task or item. At times it is frustrating. It would be nice to be able to do one thing and follow it all the way through again. Now I have to rely on others to do that.

"The learning process starts as you get out of school, and one of the things I enjoy greatly about moving up is the opportunity to train the younger engineers right out of school. So although I'm not out in the field as much as I used to be, I am teaching and sharing my experiences with people who are out in the field."

O'Brien advises those interested in this career to "develop strong math, science, and problem-solving skills. You will need problem-solving skills throughout an entire engineering career, whatever field of engineering you may be in. An extremely inquisitive mind is also vital to performing adequately in this field."

See Geotechnical Engineering, page 99.

Chapter 7

Marine Careers

All at last return to the sea—to Oceanus, the ocean river, like the ever flowing stream of time, the beginning and the end.
Rachel Carson

Oceans are vital to our lives in many ways: They are the ultimate source of water on earth, a source of food, and a means of transportation. The importance of the sea was recognized by the United Nations when it designated 1998 as the International Year of the Ocean. During the year, conferences and other events were held to raise awareness and gain a greater understanding of the oceans and issues relating to them. The Web site of the National Ocean Conference, held in California on June 11 and 12, 1998, describes the importance of oceans in these words:

Oceans sustain life on Earth and provide us with many vital resources. They are a source of food, energy, commerce, medicine, and recreation. They shape our weather, link us to other nations, and are critical to our national security. In the 21st century, we will look increasingly to the ocean to meet our everyday needs.

Our lives are inextricably linked to the ocean. One of every six jobs in the United States is marine related, and one-third of our gross domestic product is produced in the coastal zone through fishing, transportation, recreation, and other industries. Our national security and foreign trade are dependent on preserving freedom of navigation on the high seas for military and commercial vessels worldwide.

Many individuals, however, are attracted to the sea and work there because of a sheer love of water and the marine environment. Some of these individuals may seek a career in oceanography (covered in chapter 5), which involves graduate study as well as research. For others it may mean working on ships, as a diver, or in the fishing industry; this chapter covers these career possibilities.

Ships offer a great variety of positions. Many are not in the outdoors, although the deck positions do involve outdoor work. You can work on a commercial ship that is part of the U.S. merchant marine, in the U.S. armed services (Coast Guard or Navy), or in the Royal Canadian Navy.

Commercial diving may also involve work in the sea; although some commercial diving takes place in inland bodies of water, a great deal is in the marine environment. The fishing industry and related careers are also covered in this chapter.

MERCHANT MARINE

Salary Range	Varies, depending on the position; begins at around $175 per week, averages about $600 per week, and tops off at about $1,500 per week
Educational Requirements	Some postsecondary training; the amount of training depends on the position
Employment Outlook	Slower than average

The merchant marine, also known as the commercial shipping industry, transports cargo or passengers by means of water on domestic or international routes. Merchant marine careers cover the multiplicity of tasks needed to keep a ship going. They fall into four basic divisions. The *deck group* is in charge of the navigation and handling of the ship; the *engine group* keeps the ship in operation, which includes making any necessary repairs; the *purser group* handles business and accounting; and the *steward group* takes care of meals and living quarters.

Life on board ship is quite different from any other type of work. It is confining; staffers can leave only when the ship is in port and they are off duty. Because of duties relating to loading or unloading the cargo, leave may be difficult to obtain.

Older and smaller ships have more limited living areas—which might mean sharing rooms and bathrooms—and less spacious recreation facilities. Private rooms, air-conditioning, and television are standard features of new ships, however.

The length of voyages varies considerably, from several weeks to many months, depending on whether the ship travels internationally or on inland waterways. Basically, however, deck officers and sailors spend most of their time away from their homes and families.

A good way to become qualified is to attend a maritime school, such as the Massachusetts Maritime Academy or the California Maritime Academy. To attend the U.S. Merchant Marine Academy, you must be nominated by a member of the U.S. Congress.

A high school diploma is not needed for lower-level seaman jobs, but high school graduates will have an edge in getting positions and moving up within the ranks. Engineers and deck officers must have graduated from accredited nautical schools, most of which offer four-year programs.

The outlook for work in this career is very limited. New technology and new automated equipment are performing work formerly done by people, so fewer workers are now needed. Competition for the jobs opened up when staff members leave is quite keen.

The U.S. Coast Guard does the licensing and documentation of all merchant mariners in the United States. If you're seeking seafaring employment, contact the nearest U.S. Coast Guard Regional Examination Center or the Royal Canadian Navy to obtain local advice and information about regulations.

Deck Group

The captain, sometimes called a master, is the highest-ranking officer on the ship. As such, he or she is ultimately responsible for the ship, all workers on the ship, and all operations of the ship. A captain is the administrator who oversees all work, represents the shipowner, and also does some navigating as a check on the work of the ship's officers. This immensely responsible position includes making decisions about saving a ship in trouble at sea, ordering supplies and services for the ship, and ensuring safe working conditions for the crew. In port the captain must clear the vessel through customs and may need to contact the consulate or discuss business with agents of the owner in foreign ports.

Chief mates, also known as first mates or chief officers, assist the captain and are in charge of the other deck officers. They also oversee the loading and unloading of cargo. Each mate is assigned a four-hour watch, during which he or she navigates the ship. During this time, the mate follows the captain's orders about speed and course. Chief mates also record the ship's position at given times, post lookouts, and record their watches in the ship's log. If anything unusual happens, they must tell the captain immediately.

Second mates have special navigation duties. They not only check the instruments every day and keep the navigation charts updated, but also maintain and repair navigation equipment. Like chief mates, each second mate is assigned a four-hour watch.

The lowest-ranking deck officers are the third mates, usually the licensed officers with the least experience. They assist the chief mate in supervising cargo loading and unloading, ensure that the lifeboats and other lifesaving equipment are ready for emergency use, and figure the ship's position.

The radio officer operates, maintains, and repairs the radio and all other electronic communication devices, such as depth-recording equipment and radar. The radio officer also receives and keeps records of time signals, position reports, weather reports, and other important data.

Although deck officers live and work in comfortable quarters with their own rooms or cabins, working outdoors means that they experience all types of weather on board ship, from tropical heat to subfreezing cold, as well as storms at sea. They also spend weeks or months at a time away from home.

Deck officers must pass examinations to work at any of these levels. These examinations draw upon their experience as they work up from third to first mate. Third-mate applicants must either have had a minimum of three years' experience at sea or have graduated from an approved maritime school. These four-year programs give a solid grounding in the skills needed to handle a ship and include other related courses, such as construction, engineering, and law, as well as liberal arts.

The entry-level deck job is the ordinary seaman—an unskilled worker who does general maintenance work. The next step up is the able seaman, who takes two-hour turns at steering the ship, does general upkeep work, handles deck equipment and all gear, and practices fire prevention and firefighting methods.

Able seamen with experience can advance to the position of quartermaster, which involves navigation and being in charge of the ship when in port. The highest-ranking seamen are the boatswains; they take orders directly from the ship's officers and supervise the other deck seamen.

Engine Group

The chief engineers preside over the engine group, which operates and maintains the engines and other ship machinery. They oversee the engine area—including the boiler room and the electrical, refrigeration, and heating systems—in addition to sanitary systems and water supplies. Repairs, replacement of parts, and fire prevention and control are also part of their job.

The next level down in the engineering department consists of the first assistant engineers. They supervise the crew in tasks such as starting, stopping, and controlling the speed of the main engines, and they repair and maintain the engines and other ship machinery. Below them are the second assistant engineers, who monitor the water levels, steam pressure, and oil and water temperatures in the boilers, condensers, and evaporators. Next are the third assistant engineers, who supervise the engine room operation and the vessel's pumps.

Other engine-related tasks are performed by oilers, who keep moving parts of engines and equipment greased and lubricated; firemen-watertenders, who ensure that the steam pressure remains constant; wipers, who clean machinery and boilers; electricians, who maintain and repair electrical equipment; and refrigeration engineers, who maintain refrigeration equipment for perishable cargoes.

Unlike deck workers, who experience all kinds of weather on deck, the engine room staff works indoors around hot engines and equipment.

Purser Group
The purser group handles paperwork such as payroll, tariffs, customs, and payment for supplies. Pursers may also handle clerical work for other departments of the ship. On smaller ships the captain handles this work.

Steward Group
The steward group is responsible for preparing and serving meals and maintaining the living quarters. The chief steward, who plans meals and orders food, supervises the other staff, which includes chief cook, baker, and mess staff.

FISHING

Salary Range   Varies from $9,000 to an average of $25,000, and can top off at around $120,000 for work on large fishing vessels

Educational Requirements   None; skills are learned on the job, although courses in boat navigation, handling, safety, and engine and radio maintenance are helpful

Employment Outlook   Poor

The fishing industry is located along the seacoasts and the inland waterways. Fishers may work close to shore or may go out quite far, depending on the type of fish they pursue. They may work in small boats or on large, modern, commercial fishing ships. In recent years some individuals have found employment in the recreational charter fishing business. Some fishers rent their boats and expertise to customers who wish to go on sport fishing trips.

Fishing became a major industry early in the colonization of North America by Europeans. When discovered by the Europeans, North America had large quantities of fish and other marine life. For many communities on the coasts of the large inland lakes and of the oceans, fishing was the major livelihood.

In recent years the fishing industry has undergone great changes. Many fishing areas have faced great problems with pollution. Some traditional fishing grounds, especially off the East Coast, have faced problems of declining fish stocks. Much of this decline can be traced to the large commercial fishing fleets that now dominate a market previously ruled by family fishing boats. Government restrictions aimed at preserving these rich fishing grounds are a current reality for all individuals who fish.

Fishers who work bays or harbors or who go out in the morning and return by evening usually fish alone and in small boats no longer than sixty feet. They sometimes use hooks and lines to fish, although nets and traps are more common. Some may dig for clams and oysters in the sand in bays or use traps to catch crabs and lobsters.

Offshore or deep-sea fishing takes place 5 to 150 miles from the shore. The ships are usually sixty to two hundred feet long and equipped with refrigerated holds to keep the catch fresh until they return to shore. The fisher traps schools of fish in nets and scoops the trapped fish into the hold. Large ships may remain at sea for many weeks, traveling to find good fishing grounds.

To be in business as a fisher requires a high initial outlay for a boat and equipment. And the outlook for the industry is not good. Overfishing has decreased harvests; the high cost of getting into and staying in business has forced some people out and discouraged others from entering. And although the demand for fish is increasing, a lot of it is being filled by the commercial fisheries industry.

The work is hard, entailing much lifting of heavy fish and equipment. Working and living quarters at sea are usually cramped. Fishers also face the hazard of bad weather at sea, although good radios and modern navigational equipment have made the work less dangerous than it previously was. Yet this industry, difficult and dangerous as it can be, is still attractive to those lured by the romance, charm, and excitement of working on the waters under the open sky.

COMMERCIAL FISHERIES

Salary Range	Varies, depending on educational requirements and size of company
Educational Requirements	Range from none to a master's degree or doctorate
Employment Outlook	Good

East Asia leads the world in the number of commercial fisheries, with about 70 percent of them; production there concentrates on finfish and seaweed. West Asia is second with about 12 percent of world production, and other countries are becoming more active in this important industry.

Commercial fisheries in the United States began in the 1920s and 1930s with a focus on fish for bait. However, they have grown rapidly, especially in the South, as the demand for fish has increased. And the type of fish grown has expanded to include catfish, crayfish, salmon, trout, and oysters—fish that are used for eating. Expansion is likely to continue in the future, for fish consumption is increasing at the same time as the natural supply of fish is shrinking. The major limitation on growth tends to be a lack of appropriate water supplies and a proper means of handling effluents, although aquaculture can be quite simple and cheap—for example, using a farm pond. This is a complicated industry, however, and issues such as disease require close monitoring.

Fisheries face many problems today. Water use—dredging, dams, or withdrawal for industrial or agricultural purposes—can change the water habitat, either killing fish or interfering with reproduction. Water pollution and overfishing pose grave threats to many fisheries.

Fisheries provide challenging and varied careers, with many options to pursue. Some possible positions are research biologist, fisheries manager, aquaculturist, fish production technician, and administrator.

Each career within the fisheries field has its specific requirements. Some, especially in research areas and educational institutions, require advanced training, up to a doctorate. A minimal background for most other positions is a bachelor's degree in fisheries science, aquatic ecology, or a closely related field. Although a fish production technician may need only a high school diploma, some positions prefer at least two years of college; more college work is a real advantage, especially for those who wish to advance in the field. Recently, a master's degree has been required for some entry-level research and management positions in government and private organizations.

Research

Research biologists who work with fisheries study water organisms and how they interact with their environment. They may examine ways that recreational and commercial activities affect the fishery population, and relationships between aquatic resources and humans. Research is a key ingredient in the management of fisheries resources.

Research areas include genetics, the study of genes and how they produce similarities and differences among species; limnology, the study of plant and animal life in bodies of fresh water such as lakes and ponds; marine biology, the study of organisms living in the sea; pathology, the study of the origins, nature, causes, and development of disease; and physiology, the study of the proper functioning of animals and plants under different conditions.

Research scientists will need broad training in areas such as biology, ecology, statistics, and mathematics, as well as good communications skills. In-depth research in any of these areas will require a great deal of specific knowledge and probably graduate study.

The major employers of fisheries biologists in the United States and Canada are federal and state or provincial fish and wildlife agencies. International job opportunities, particularly in developing nations, can be found through agencies such as the Peace Corps or the United Nations Food and Agricultural Organization. Other employment opportunities can be found with universities, power companies, the fisheries industry, environmental consulting firms, and nonprofit organizations. Pay for research scientists in fisheries varies widely, depending on the employer and the required background. It can range from about $25,000 to $38,000 or possibly more.

Fisheries Management

Fisheries managers use the results obtained from research to improve the various aspects of a fishery. For example, they may wish to use the study of genetics and physiology to increase the numbers or size of the fish that are harvested. Managers organize and implement fish-stocking programs; they also enforce regulations pertaining to fishing or harvest and access by fishers. They may interview fishers to gather data helpful in the development of fisheries. Public relations is also an important part of fisheries management.

One area of study that is helpful to fisheries managers is biology; in addition, those interested in becoming managers should study communications, public policy and administration, and sociology. Pay varies tremendously, depending upon the setting, but it averages $40,000 to $50,000.

Aquaculture

Aquaculturists are the people in the fisheries industry who have the job of actually producing the fish or shellfish. It is important that they know the physiological, nutritional, and environmental needs of the organism being raised, whether it is catfish, crayfish, trout, salmon, oysters, or shrimp. Most fisheries have a fairly high fish density and are quite susceptible to outbreaks of disease; aquaculturists must be familiar with the diseases and health problems of the species being raised.

An aquaculturist's background should include biology and specific study of fish, including nutrition and health. Also important is a knowledge of water chemistry, genetics, and business operations, as well as market economics.

Starting salaries are in the $20,000 to $28,000 category; with experience, pay can reach the upper $30,000 range.

See Profile, page 126.

Fish Production Technologist

Fish production technologists are employed in different settings. Some technicians work in private companies (or fish farms) that produce fish to be used as food for humans or animals. Others work in government-operated hatcheries that produce fish stocks for release in bodies of water where sport anglers will fish for them. The duties of the technicians vary according to the type of setting where they work.

Work that will be done in both settings, however, includes feeding the fish, clearing out sick or dead fish, monitoring and recording water conditions in tanks or ponds, and maintaining the equipment that regulates the water. Technicians are responsible for artificial breeding of the fish and inspection of the eggs. Some technicians assist biologists in their research, and others tag fish that are to be released into the wild. When the fish are caught, these tags will go back to the hatchery and the technicians will study the factors affecting the health and survival of these fish.

A great deal of the work is intricate and repetitive, and patience is necessary. Much of the work is done outdoors. This is a growing field, and individuals with more education have a distinct possibility of advancement. The pay begins at around $20,000 and tops off at about $30,000.

Fisheries Administration

Another important fisheries career is administration. The administrator oversees, plans, and coordinates the work of other people in fisheries. Some of the administrator's tasks are developing and writing laws, regulations, and policies. The administrator's work in coordinating objectives, preparing budgets, and supervising staff helps in developing priorities among the many research and management activities. The administrator needs to understand the overall relationships among the fishery, the government agency responsible for fisheries, and the public.

These senior-level management positions, which may be in state or federal government or with private organizations, are held by people with a great deal of experience in the field. Managing and research often provide good background experience for senior administrators. The pay, depending upon the organization or government setting, averages about $60,000.

COMMERCIAL DIVING

Salary Range	Starting about $15,000, averaging about $30,000, and topping off at about $52,000
Educational Requirements	Special training courses, many of which are more than thirty weeks in length
Employment Outlook	Above average

Commercial divers work underwater in both fresh water and oceans. Divers specialize in the areas of underwater welding, emergency medical care, inspection of underwater work, and nondestructive testing. They work in construction, salvage, ship repair or service, or offshore oil. This type of work demands a high level of skill and great physical strength. The tasks and settings are varied and challenging.

Some divers specialize in underwater wet welding. Special training is required to learn the techniques of underwater burning and the technology of wet shielded-arc welding.

Other divers perform underwater inspection and nondestructive testing. They may clean underwater steel structures, look for and weld defects in steel and concrete structures, and do underwater surveying. Training includes underwater photography, preparing technical inspection reports, and using ultrasonic and magnetic particle inspection equipment.

Treatment of injuries and diseases related to diving is the focus of medical technicians. Always on hand during diving operations, the emergency medical diver must know how to respond to a variety of medical emergencies and be able to stabilize a patient's condition until more extensively trained medical authorities can arrive.

Among the varied settings where commercial divers work, oil-field work is expanding and requires a great deal of skill. In this work divers are used in exploring, drilling, and producing and shipping the oil. Divers working in marine construction do almost any type of underwater work, such as inspecting and repairing breakwaters, pipelines, floating drydocks, bridge foundations, piers, and marine ways.

Salvage work demands many underwater skills, such as the use of underwater metal-cutting equipment and pneumatic, power velocity, and hydraulic tools. It also requires knowledge of ships, cargoes, and how cargoes are loaded. Dams offer many diving jobs that require more skills than most other underwater work, including surveying, inspection, some of the actual construction, and some repair work on all types of dams. Finally, commercial divers may perform inland work in locations such as rivers, harbors, lakes, and ponds that are part of power systems.

Because the work is strenuous and the setting quite alien (cold water, waves, darkness, currents, and pressure), a diver must be strong, in excellent physical and mental condition, and able to take the strain this setting presents.

Commercial diving courses take about thirty-four weeks. A high school diploma (or educational and background experience equivalent to that of a high school graduate) is a prerequisite for admission. Essential for the career is the ability to follow written instructions, make calculations, understand and follow blueprint instructions, and write intelligent reports of what was found and what is recommended. A commercial diver must have a technological background, electric and electronic experience, engineering training, and organizational ability.

Because commercial diving involves underwater mechanics, divers must have strong abilities in many mechanical fields. To perform their work, they must be able to use cutting and welding equipment and to adapt above-water tools and fittings to underwater jobs. They must also understand hydraulics and compressed air and be able to adapt these power sources to underwater tasks.

This field, already expanding before the Iraqi devastation of Kuwait, offered great potential for expansion in the 1990s, when that man-made disaster opened up a demand for commercial divers experienced in repair work. Additionally, the awareness of an overdependence on foreign oil has begun the push for more domestic oil suppliers, and the U.S. government has begun to subsidize deeper oil drilling. Aging structures also require more inspection and maintenance. As underwater technologies have developed—divers can now work at deeper levels for longer periods of time, for instance—more jobs have opened up.

Exploration for diamonds on the seafloor began in the late 1990s. Mining diamonds from the seafloor will likely open up some potential diving work in the future. The best location for this type of work is currently off the coast of South Africa, but potential for underwater diamond mining exists around the globe. Some of the areas with the most promise are Indonesia, Namibia, Ghana, Finland, the waters north of Australia, and deep Canadian waters.

As technological advances continue to fuel underwater exploration, operators of remotely operated vehicles (ROVs) can expect to have more work. This is a relatively new area within the underwater industry.

Commercial divers do not work full time. Depending on their jobs, they typically work 60 percent of the time, or about 160 days a year. For steady employment the diver must travel, following his or her employer, or search for a new job when one is completed.

See Profile, page 128.

RESOURCES

Commercial Diving

College of Oceaneering
Los Angeles Harbor
272 South Fries Avenue
Wilmington, CA 90744-6399
Telephone: 310-834-2501
Fax: 310-834-7132
Web: http://www.diveco.com

Marine Diving Technology Department
Santa Barbara City College
721 Cliff Drive
Santa Barbara, CA 93109
Telephone: 805-965-0581
Fax: 805-963-7222
Web: http://www.sbcc.cc.ca.us/

Explore UnderWater magazine
Web: http://www.exploreuw.com/aindex2.htm

Fisheries

American Fisheries Society
5410 Grosvenor Lane, Suite 110
Bethesda, MD 20814-2199
Telephone: 301-897-8616
Fax: 301-897-8096
Web: http://www.esd.ornl.gov.AFS

Aquaculture Association of Canada
Box 1987
St. Andrews, NB E0G 2X0
Telephone: 506-529-4766
Fax: 506-529-4609
Web: http://www.ifmt.nf.ca/mi/aac/ac.htm

Aquaculture magazine
Web: http://www.ioa.com/~aquamag/

Merchant Marine

U.S. Maritime Service Veterans
P.O. Box 2361
Berkeley, CA 94702-0361
Web: http://www.usmm.org/

Profile

AQUACULTURIST
Connie Young-Dubovsky

"Aquaculture is a new industry—it's exciting to be in on something new," says Connie Young-Dubovsky eagerly. "People in this field are very enthusiastic and see lots of possibilities. I'm in on the cutting edge—people don't say, 'This is the way it's always been done.'"

Young-Dubovsky is an aquaculture agent with a state cooperative extension service. Previously she worked as a fish hatchery superintendent at a North Carolina state fish hatchery and as a research assistant at Mississippi State University.

At Mississippi State she worked as a "right-hand woman," running all the research projects, including a USDA-funded grant to study the feasibility of raising hybrid striped bass in Mississippi to supplement the catfish industry. She also worked with the well-established catfish industry, trying to produce a bigger fish in a shorter amount of time. She gathered data, analyzed statistics, and wrote reports of the results. In the process, she says, "I got to handle a lot of fish in both outdoor ponds and indoor tanks."

As a fish hatchery superintendent, Young-Dubovsky was responsible for producing striped and hybrid striped bass, largemouth bass, channel catfish, and various species of sunfish for stocking state waterways and impoundments. The experience gave her a chance to apply research to a practical, hands-on situation. The job was a good transition into extension work, which bridges the theoretical and the practical.

Although Young-Dubovsky has enjoyed all of her jobs, she is most enthusiastic about the educational aspect of extension work. "Before I obtained this position I had been working on a teaching certificate, because I'm very interested in conservation education," she explains. "Part of being an aquaculture extension agent involves working with conservation education. I give information on the telephone and work on educational programs for schools and local groups.

"Aquaculture is not just fish hatcheries, as many people think. It really is agriculture—farming fish—and as such it is increasingly coming under the jurisdiction of the U.S. Department of Agriculture."

Young-Dubovsky got into fisheries by the process of elimination. When she obtained her bachelor's degree in animal science, she intended to enter veterinary school. When she wasn't accepted, though, she pursued her interest in fish and obtained a master's degree in fisheries and wildlife.

Her educational background is essential for the work she's doing, she explains. "In my position I need a master's." You can take different routes to work in fisheries, however. Some other options are agricultural engineering, agricultural economics—"an important field as the industry expands"—and biology. She chose her particular path because of her interest in biology.

Young-Dubovsky says there is no such thing as a typical day in her present position. On a recent day she visited some entrepreneurial fish farmers who have been raising catfish and another farmer who recently began stocking trout in a flow-through pond. Their fish had been dying for unknown reasons, so she took some samples of both trout and catfish to a pathology lab.

She spends a lot of time visiting and assisting local fish farmers. "I helped a local farmer, who wanted to raise crayfish, by testing his farm pond water. I also recently helped a catfish farmer examine the possibilities for restocking his farm.

"Many of the problems I deal with relate to a fish kill, the water quality, or helping farmers learn about the possibilities for changing their programs. Disease is a real problem in aquaculture. I'm not a disease specialist, but I take specimens to the lab, where vets trained in fish pathology will take over."

Young-Dubovsky also spends a lot of time in her office answering questions by telephone and obtaining necessary information. "An important personality trait for my position is being a people person—you need to like interacting with people," she says. "Because there are very few women in these positions I have to make more of an effort to establish my credibility."

One negative she has encountered is that her jobs, especially the hatchery position, have involved extra hours. "The state fish hatchery position was very intensive, not an eight-to-five job," she says. "I need more diversity in my life with time off for myself.

"One piece of advice I can give anyone interested in this career is to get as much experience as possible. Even if you volunteer or work for room and board, experience is more valuable than anything else—you need to get your feet wet. Because contacts are important, you should also attend professional meetings and meet people in the field."

See Aquaculture, page 121.

Profile

COMMERCIAL DIVER
Tom Mosher

Tom Mosher has a love-hate relationship with his career. "I love diving," he says emphatically, "but I hate the politics of the diving industry.

"I like being underwater and doing the challenging things we do underwater," he elaborates. "We are expected to accomplish tasks the average person wouldn't do." Yet he dislikes the politics involved in getting jobs, and he's seen people fired from jobs with no reason given. "Luck— being available when someone is needed—plays a greater role in finding diving jobs than your skills," he says.

Worksites for divers can be inland or offshore. Inland divers work in rivers, lakes, sewers, power plants, and on dams. For example, intakes made of concrete and steel supply water from a river or lake for industrial water uses and have filters that need to be inspected, repaired, and replaced continually. Offshore divers work in the ocean "from the beach out"—much of the work involves exploration for and production of oil and gas. Work for offshore divers is more varied as well as more dangerous than that of inshore divers.

Divers receive hourly wages plus additional pay for penetration and depth dives. On penetration dives—when they enter a confined space such as a pipeline and can't surface immediately—they are paid by the horizontal foot. For depth work, the extra pay is by the vertical foot. "With depth pay you can earn close to $1,000 a day on a 950-foot dive," Mosher says. This extra pay helps to compensate for the added danger and the time divers must take to decompress from depth dives. For example, in saturation dives every hundred feet requires a day to decompress. "Ten days in the decompression chamber can be pretty boring," Mosher says matter-of-factly.

Mosher doesn't talk a great deal about danger, but he does say that in a recent six-month job he was almost killed three times and got the bends three times. (*Bends* is a nickname for decompression sickness, which occurs when a diver exceeds the time limit at a specific depth.)

Mosher has worked both inland and offshore: "I prefer diving offshore but I don't like the lifestyle as much—it is much harder to stay healthy. Offshore we work very irregular hours. We never know when we will dive. Inland we work more regular hours."

Because of the skills required and dangers involved in offshore work, divers serve an apprenticeship as "tenders" for two to four years before being allowed to work offshore as divers. A tender essentially takes care of the divers, tending to hose while they are underwater and carrying supplies while they are in the decompression chamber. They also do dirty work such as deck cleanup. Mosher says tenders generally are not treated well and earn from $5 to $9 an hour, compared with the $10 to $17 hourly rate that divers receive. Tenders do some diving, depending on their skill level, and it is their skill that determines when they "break out" as divers.

According to Mosher, ideal candidates for diving positions are twenty-two years old, single, and have a construction background and mechanical aptitude. "You travel a lot in commercial diving to find jobs, and you don't have a guaranteed income," he explains. "At the beginning you can be very poor. This kind of life wreaks havoc on building or keeping relationships. The divorce rate in the diving industry is extremely high. If you don't want a family or a settled life, then this kind of life is fine."

Mosher believes one of the most important traits commercial divers need is something that can't be taught—common sense. "Divers need to be able to look at things, see what needs to be done, and do it," he explains. "A few commercial divers haven't been to dive school. If I were to do it again, I would consider the option of finding the least-expensive school that would give an air certificate." (An air certificate allows a diver to work using tanks containing only oxygen, at depths to about 190 feet; for dives deeper than 190 feet, a diver must have another certificate allowing the use of mixed gases.)

Mosher hasn't met many women divers. "Diving has its good moments, but it is cold, dirty, and hard work," he explains. "You will get dirtier than you ever believed you would get. It's a very hard lifestyle—physically and emotionally demanding. You may deal with the whole range of emotions in one day—from fear to exhilaration—and it can be emotionally exhausting. We get up at odd hours and deal with miseries from being very cold to very hot. It's not a lifestyle most women would be a part of.

"As long as man is working near or on the water there will always be a need for divers," Mosher states. He adds: "Diving is hard, dangerous, dirty work, and your chances of succeeding as a professional diver are slim because it's definitely not a career for everyone. You should not get into diving for the money, but because you love working on or in the water."

See Commercial Diving, page 122.

Chapter 8

Recreation

If all the year were playing holidays,
To sport would be as tedious as to work.
William Shakespeare, *King Henry IV*

A s the new millennium opens, organized recreation has increased in importance. At least two factors have contributed to this. One is a decrease (at least in some fields) in the total number of working hours, which has given the workforce additional leisure time. The second factor is the increase in the numbers of healthy and vigorous retired people. In fact, career publications in the late 1990s note that leisure services is among the fastest-growing job sectors—expanding at a rate of 5 percent or more per year.

With the growing prominence of organized recreation has come more jobs for recreation workers, who are involved in planning, organizing, and directing these leisure activities. Outdoor employment is available in sports and organized recreation activities, camping, hunting, fishing, sightseeing, and nature-oriented activities.

The types of employers vary widely. More than half of all recreation workers are employed by governments, primarily at the municipal and county levels, although many work in state park systems and for some federal programs. Many others work in membership organizations, including the YWCA, the Girl Scouts, and the Red Cross. Social-service organizations (such as senior centers) and residential care facilities (such as group homes and halfway houses) also provide jobs in recreation. Other employers can range from wilderness and survival organizations to sports and entertainment centers, camps, travel agencies, companies specializing in vacation trips, hotels and resorts, and apartment complexes.

The settings for recreation programs vary as widely as do the employers and include pristine wilderness areas, city parks, health clubs, and cruise ships. While there are some exceptions—wilderness trips, for example—job locations generally coincide with population centers; the majority of the jobs are in urban or suburban areas, or in camps in states or provinces with higher populations.

Many recreation positions are full time, but you'll find very strong components of part-time or weekend work and a hefty increase of workers in the summertime. There are also many opportunities for volunteer work. In the recreation field, part-time and volunteer work often leads to full-time positions. Occasionally, it is even possible to find satisfactory full-time employment in outdoor recreation by combining several careers. For example, a high school environment teacher might spend the summer teaching wilderness survival skills. A ski patroller may work in the off season on ski trails or ski lift maintenance and construction. It is even possible to combine writing and tour- boat guiding, as the profile of Tim Jones in this chapter demonstrates (see page 150). Considering the variety of positions in recreation, you can creatively combine several to suit your preferred lifestyle.

Because the careers are so diverse, educational requirements vary widely. Many summer positions don't even require a high school diploma, while many administrative positions require graduate education. College graduates with majors in recreation, leisure studies, or parks fill many career positions, but the job requirements in the private sector may simply be a bachelor's degree and aptitude or experience. Specialized skills and certificates are required for many jobs, such as diving or lifesaving.

CAMPING CAREERS

Salary Range	Varies depending on size of camp and position; a director in a small camp may earn $24,000 to $26,500, while a director in a larger camp might earn $30,000 to $40,000
Educational Requirements	Usually a bachelor's degree, and often graduate work for career camping positions

Employment Outlook   Good; with the move to specialty camps such as equestrian or tennis, more opportunities are opening

Camps differ tremendously in size and focus; this determines the types of positions at each. Generally all positions, except some in administration, are seasonal; this does, however, depend on the focus of the camp. The current trend in camping is toward more full-time positions. Another trend is toward camps that offer programs encompassing all ages—children, youth, adults, and senior citizens—either in different time periods or at the same time in family settings. Settings themselves vary from day to residential camps; also, camps are no longer strictly a phenomenon of the summer months.

Camping positions call for a great variety of backgrounds and disciplines. They use the principles of social work, psychology, physical education, recreation, and education. They also call for skills in business management, nutrition and food service, and repair and maintenance of buildings.

Career positions in camping include camp administrator, who is in charge of several camp programs; camp director, who heads the administration and program of a specific camp; associate director, who assists the administrator and often directs the camp program; outdoor program director, who coordinates, plans, and administers a specific outdoor program; and trip leader (this title varies), who leads groups on extended outdoor experiences.

The camp administrator often works in a metropolitan area and only visits the camps from time to time. The director usually stays at a resident campsite year-round.

CAREERS IN RECREATION

Salary Range   Varies widely, depending on position, geographic location, experience and education, and the number of staff; beginning salaries are about $12,000 to $20,000 a year; recreation director and other administrators range from $22,000 to $95,000, averaging $43,000; full-time swimming instructors make about $13,800 to $17,500, and part-time swimming instructors $4.50 to $8.50 an hour

Educational Requirements   High school plus training, depending on the specifics of the job; for example,

swimming instructors usually need Red
Cross and advanced lifesaving certification

Employment Outlook   Very good

In the past, many people considered organized recreation services as glorified fun-and-games operations whose main concern was providing programs of hobbies, sports, or games. In reality, recreation administration is an extremely responsible and varied position, involving far more than fun and games. Administrators usually oversee the operations of entire agencies, either in the public or private sector, and are responsible for the budgeting, marketing, and trend forecasting. In essence, the recreation administrator is responsible for helping individuals enjoy their leisure time by providing opportunities to relax, socialize, and exercise.

The jobs available in this field are totally dependent on the setting. Still, they include the following: director of recreation and parks, recreation supervisor, recreation center director, recreation leader, recreation workers (including swimming instructors), and park planners.

Administrative positions are mostly held by college graduates who have majored in fields such as recreation and leisure studies, physical education, parks, and fitness management. Academic studies and experience are generally minimum requirements for administration jobs and give you more possibilities for advancement. Master's degrees in parks, recreation, leisure studies, and related disciplines are now becoming more common.

Many swimming instructors work at outdoor pools. The disadvantages of this type of setting include, of course, the dangers of sun damage and sunstroke. Swimming instruction is also both physically and mentally demanding. For example, instructors will teach students at all ages and skill levels. Summer positions may pay slightly less, but include the benefits of room and board.

The employment outlook in recreation is considered very good, although many positions will be as replacements for individuals leaving or retiring from the field. Still, considering the increasing numbers of retirees—and their interest in leisure services—along with the continuing interest in fitness and health issues, this field should remain fairly stable for the foreseeable future.

Constraints on recreation positions are usually due to local government budget restrictions. In fact, the potential for more part-time positions in this field exists, because that is one way to deal with budget problems. Unfortunately, these types of services are affected by the overall health of the economy—although the rising clout of senior citizens may prevent too much attrition in the industry.

Career opportunities and salaries in this field are quite dependent on the region and the local economic situation. Competition for jobs is also quite keen, and this is expected to continue. To gain an edge in qualifications for both supervisory and administrative positions, individuals will need experience and formal training in the recreation field.

CRUISE SHIP POSITIONS

Salary Range	Varies greatly, depending on the specific job, required background, and ship size, but ranges from $500 a week to $2,500 (on the largest ships) and includes accommodations and food
Educational Requirements	Depend on the specific jobs performed
Employment Outlook	Fair

Cruise ships can be exciting places to work, because they present the opportunity to travel to different places, although staff and crew members often have little time to go ashore. Cruise ships offer a variety of jobs, few of which match exactly the positions shown on the popular television show *The Love Boat*. In fact, those interested in cruise ship jobs should be aware that they are not easy. The work is usually hard, the hours long, and the positions difficult to obtain. The work focuses on the safety and happiness of the passengers, and everyone working on board who has any contact with the passengers is expected to keep this in mind. Friendliness and the ability to get along well with others are essential assets in cruise ship positions. Jobs fall into two categories: staff and crew. Staff members include the cruise director and cruise staff, who are responsible for ship activities and excursions onshore; entertainers, such as musicians, singers, dancers, magicians, and comedians; and sometimes lecturers, fitness and recreational specialists, or people who handle children's activities or arts and crafts. In general, staff members have more contact with the passengers than crew members do.

Numbered among the crew workers are the cabin stewards, who keep the cabins clean; the deck stewards, who clean and serve food; and the bar stewards, who serve drinks. Waiters and busboys clean the dining areas and serve food, and the kitchen crew prepares the food. Hairdressers and boutique and casino operators may also be part of the crew.

All workers on cruise ships work seven days a week; vacation time varies, depending on the specific job. The staff positions have fairly high burnout rates; typically, staffers spend about three years in these positions. Those who stay longer can work their way into cruise director careers.

Being able to speak a number of languages is an asset for cruise ship staff. A good knowledge of recreational activities and fitness is important, as is the capacity to live in a situation with little privacy. Ability to work on a moving ship, especially when the seas are rough, is essential. Because of job competition, the best strategy is to either work through agencies that recruit staff for cruise ships or contact the cruise line directly. A bonus of these jobs is that some of the earnings may be tax-free, because a great deal of the work on a cruise ship is performed outside the country of origin.

Staff

The cruise director oversees all shipboard activities (entertainment, fitness, hairdressing, boutiques, and casinos) and onshore excursions. Duties include supervising staffers who organize walks, aerobics, contests, and movies, as well as the lecturers. Onshore excursions involve many small details to sort out and problems to solve, including checking to make sure that port services still meet expectations. Working hours usually begin at 7 a.m. and may continue to 1 a.m., with some time off during the day.

Entertainers perform a certain number of shows per cruise; on smaller ships they may be involved with other shipboard or onshore activities.

Crew

Cabin stewards keep cabins clean and supplied in addition to serving food and drinks to passengers in cabins. They are able to go onshore on a rotating basis but often spend free time sleeping. These employees begin work at about 6 a.m. and end at 10 p.m., with some time off during the day. Waiters must be able to tell passengers the ingredients of the items on the menu, take the orders, and serve the food. They must be sensitive to passenger tastes and substitute another dish if what is served is not satisfactory.

The main responsibilities of busboys are clearing the tables and refilling water glasses and coffee cups. They also assist waiters in bringing food out of the kitchen. A waiter may serve about five tables, and a busboy ten. Following are typical hours for both waiters and busboys: 6 a.m. to 10 a.m., 11 a.m. to 3 p.m., and 5:30 p.m. to 10 p.m. Another shift, from 11 p.m. to 1:30 a.m., is generally rotated among workers. There is very little time off.

Bar stewards take orders for drinks and serve them, which allows for plenty of time to interact with passengers. Stewards usually work one of two shifts: 9 a.m. to 5 p.m., or 4 p.m. to 1 or 2 a.m.

DIVING INSTRUCTION

Salary Range	Depends on position; full-time instructors at retail facilities start at about $15,000 and can earn as much as $40,000 to $50,000; owners of stores or resorts can make more
Educational Requirements	Certification to teach diving
Employment Outlook	Excellent

Scuba diving is another recreational pursuit that provides opportunities for outdoor careers. Because of the dangers of underwater diving, recreational scuba divers must be certified. This certification comes from organizations such as the Professional Association of Diving Instructors (PADI), the National Association of Underwater Instructors (NAUI), the YMCA, and Scuba Schools International. All offer courses in diving.

Diving instruction offers opportunities to travel and to work in unusual locations. Basically, dive instructors teach the skills of diving to their students. They also work to ensure that their students remain interested in and active in the sport through additional dive travel experiences. Divers also supervise the diving activities that take place in resorts and on cruise ships. Although a resort or cruise ship setting may appear to be ideal, these jobs present their own stresses. Divers must work to fill the needs of a very diverse clientele with varying levels of skill and experience.

Underwater swimming and diving skills are the minimum essentials for this career, and a prerequisite for teaching diving instruction courses is certification to dive. Instructors must also be certified, which involves taking instructors' courses and passing an examination. Some courses qualify diving instructors to teach the popular specialties, such as wreck diving, deep diving, underwater photography, underwater navigating, search-and-recovery diving, and night diving. Rescue courses are also required for diving instructors.

PADI has developed a dive instruction course that has been recognized by the American Council on Education for college and university credit. PADI instructors are also recognized worldwide; the association's dive centers are located in more than fifty countries.

As a recreational sport, scuba diving is increasing in popularity. Previously remote areas of the world are being opened up to it. More people are considering diving a fun, relaxing recreation. Consequently, the demand for qualified dive instructors is expected to remain high. Many diving instructors work full time through dive shops; others teach on a part-time basis.

THE HORSE INDUSTRY

Salary Range	Varies; grooms from $7,800 to $13,200; riding instructors about $25 per hour; trainers start at between $14,200 and $16,200
Educational Requirements	Vary depending on the job; most entry-level positions provide on-the-job training
Employment Outlook	Fair

Increasingly at the end of the twentieth century, work attitudes have changed; individuals are beginning to place more value on quality of life than on climbing the corporate ladder. For many people, horses provide a perfect "get-away-from-it-all" mechanism. They are seen by many as an adjunct to a "Western," or more nature-centered, lifestyle. The use of horses for recreation, as a means to respond to the stresses of contemporary life, is thus increasing. This does not necessarily mean owning a horse, but it does mean having horses accessible.

Quite a variety of careers can be found in the horse industry. The level of education required ranges from a doctorate or a professional degree all the way down to a high school diploma. The level of contact with horses also ranges from daily contact or work in horse shows, rodeos, or the racing industry to infrequent contact in careers that involve issues related to horses.

Examples of careers that include daily contact with horses and a high level of education are veterinarian, geneticist, animal nutritionist, and extension specialist in horses or animals. Careers requiring slightly less education include pedigree analyst, county agriculture agent, farm or ranch manager, humane society official, and mounted police officer.

Horse shows, rodeos, and the racing industry offer positions such as horse show manager, judge, course and jump designer, publicist, security person, and photographer. Positions that require a great deal of skill and experience are jockey, trainer, driver, and rodeo rider.

A farrier, or blacksmith as this position is commonly called, takes care of a horse's hooves, trimming them, making new horseshoes, and putting on horseshoes. A farrier needs great strength in the arms and back and must be certified from an accredited school (usually a six-week, full-time course). An apprenticeship with an experienced farrier is also a definite plus.

See Profile, page 146.

OUTFITTING AND GUIDING

Salary Range	Beginning guides make $500 to $600 a month; experienced guides earn more, but pay depends on the type of hunt and difficulty in finding quarry; most guides can set their own fee schedules after they are established in the industry
Educational Requirements	Guide schools teach the basics
Employment Outlook	Fair

Because the chance to hunt or fish in the wild, or to win a trophy for the recreation room, continues to attract unskilled sportspeople, the need for professional hunting and fishing guides will continue. Guides are hired by outfitters—who are required, by most governments, to have a license before they may outfit hunting expeditions. The outfitters handle insurance and equipment and are liable for the actions of guides.

A professional guide takes sportspeople who may have no knowledge of the wilderness and helps them make a kill. Typical game varieties in demand are elk, deer, bear, antelope, and different types of fish. This profession demands a thorough knowledge of the wilderness or the waters, especially the ability to track and find animals. Not only do guides help largely unskilled outdoorspeople, but they also have to cover a fair amount of territory, usually by foot, and carry heavy loads. In bear hunting, for example, bait must be carried in, and when a shot has been successful, the trophy must be cleaned and carried out.

Guides must be able to outfit the inexperienced hunter with the proper equipment and, if necessary, know how to use pack animals. Expertise with weapons—guns, bow and arrow, or fishing rod—is essential.

Guides must also be able to work well with people. The clients who hire the services of a guide may be totally unskilled in wilderness lore, shooting, or angling; they may not even be pleasant to associate with. The guide must give each person his or her money's worth and a sense that the hunt was successful, even if the client does not come back with a trophy.

In addition to a knowledge of the woods, guides must know about the habits of animals and how to best locate the particular quarry of the hunt. Fishing guides must know about fishing, as well as river floating. Other important skills are camping and lifesaving.

In some coastal areas, such as the Chesapeake Bay, boat owners rent out their craft to individuals who want to spend a day or so deep-sea fishing. In these situations the boat must be seaworthy, and the captain and crew must be able to handle the ship, offer suggestions and help to novice fishers, and deal with any emergencies that may arise. This type of work is most in demand during the summer months.

Guides work quite hard. Hunting season usually encompasses only the months of September through November, although there may be winter hunts; fishing seasons generally run from spring through fall but vary widely with the location. (Saltwater fishing continues year-round in southern waters.) If the business is family owned or operated, you may spend more time outside—sometimes as much as six months—either guiding or scouting to prepare for the upcoming season. The continuing demand for good guides reflects the need for such a service. There is, however, a high turnover rate among guides because of the time away from home this career requires.

SKI PATROLLING

Salary Range	From $5 to $15 an hour, depending upon experience and the size of the resort
Educational Requirements	Winter emergency care and first-aid courses
Employment Outlook	Good

The main concern of ski patrollers is the safety of the skiing public. Working at ski areas, they provide first-aid and rescue services for injured or lost skiers and offer information about skiing safety. The types of background required for this job may vary slightly from ski area to ski area. Common requirements are that you have some medical training, are an expert skier, and have either experience or training in mountain rescue.

Ski patrollers typically spend about eight hours a day on the slopes, although they may work longer if there is danger of avalanches. At the beginning of each working day the patrollers are given instructions and special work assignments, which might include helping with ski races scheduled for that day, posting signs to warn of hazards, or giving special instructions.

Patrollers also ski the course before it is opened to the public to look for and smooth out ridges or piles of snow that may have been left by the huge grooming machines that work on the ski slopes every night. Signs must be checked for ice or anything else that makes them difficult to read, and patrollers must make certain that the ropes marking the boundary of the ski areas are visible. One patroller always stays at the summit head-quarters (a duty that is rotated) to answer the phone and radio. If this person needs to leave for any reason, he or she will radio for a replacement. All ski patrollers wear radios for the instant contact that is necessary in emergencies.

Avalanches are common problems for skiers, and avalanche forecast-ing, which is sometimes done through the ski resort's own weather station, is important for patrolling. If avalanche problems are suspected, patrollers go to the slopes very early in the day to defuse the situation by triggering an avalanche before skiers arrive on the slopes.

Ski patrollers must also be able to evacuate ski lifts in case of an emer-gency. This involves descending the lifts on the cables and lowering skiers by rope to the ground, which requires good physical conditioning. This career demands great skill in skiing, including the ability to ski tough ter-rain. Patrollers must have successfully completed courses in winter emer-gency procedures and cardiopulmonary resuscitation. Training in handling toboggans, lift evacuation, and other safety procedures is also required. Since ski patrolling is so physically demanding, few people stay in it for a lifetime.

Although the pay is not high, ski patrolling can be a very rewarding and fulfilling career. If you love to ski, it allows you to enjoy the sport and help others to enjoy it as well. It can, however, be a very physically and mentally taxing career.

Ski patrolling is a seasonal job from mid-November to sometime in April, depending on the location and weather. Ski patrollers usually bal-ance this career by working summer seasonal jobs such as construction. Many resorts also use volunteer patrollers to assist their professionals. Although the field reflects the economic situation of the moment, as well as weather conditions, new ski patrolling positions are available every year because of attrition.

See Profile, page 148.

SKYDIVING INSTRUCTION

Salary Range	Varies, depending on place and type of instruction; for accelerated free-fall instruction, fees are about $20 per student
Educational Requirements	Training is available through the United States Parachute Association
Employment Outlook	Growing

Essentially, a skydiving instructor teaches people how to jump out of airplanes. All instructors must be experienced sky divers who are able to teach. This industry is not regulated by the federal government, and only a few states have regulations. A majority of the sky divers, instructors, and drop zones (mainly airports where the dives take place) belong to the United States Parachute Association (USPA).

A private organization concerned with the safety of the sport, the USPA publishes a magazine that focuses on safety in skydiving. Additionally, instructors who teach at USPA drop zones must have taken USPA classes on teaching and pass written, oral, and practical tests. There are three levels of instructors: At the top is the jump-master, followed by the instructor, and then the instructor-examiner.

There are three methods of practical instruction after the student has completed a course. The static line jump is from a height of three thousand feet, and the student's parachute is activated when the student leaves the plane. In the tandem jump (also at three thousand feet), the student is a passenger, attached to the instructor at the shoulders and hips, and the instructor operates the parachute. The accelerated free fall is a jump from a height of at least ten thousand feet. The student jumps at the same time as the instructors, and they do some maneuvers before the parachute is opened. For the initial jump and levels 1 to 3, two instructors jump with each student. For levels 4 to 7, one instructor jumps with each student. This method allows for maximum instruction in practice and immediate correction if it's needed.

Skydiving is a growing sport with increasing numbers of students. Pay for instruction generally is not high, although it varies in each location. Professional instructors who work for large operations usually receive the highest wages. Many instructors teach mainly because they enjoy the work and not because they receive high pay.

Skydiving is a highly seasonal sport. The majority of the drop zones operate only on weekends in warm weather, although some few operate full time throughout the summer. In mild climates where there is a large population and good demand, it is possible to teach skydiving full time.

THE TOURISM INDUSTRY

Salary Range	Varies tremendously; tour escorts make between $325 and $550 a week, and some also receive tips
Educational Requirements	A high school diploma is the minimum; college or training courses by tour companies will aid in finding jobs
Employment Outlook	Very good

Tour companies employ drivers and tour guides as well as administrators, support staff, and salespeople. The job in the tourism industry with the most potential for outdoor work is that of tour escort or guide.

Tour escorts lead groups of people on trips, known as packaged tours, that give travelers a complete itinerary with transportation, lodging, and sight-seeing all arranged. A fringe benefit of the work for tour escorts is that they receive free travel and hotel accommodations. Some negative factors are the lengthy stays away from home and gaps in employment.

Other tour guides, known as step-on guides, meet buses and take tourists on one-day trips around a certain area. Occasionally, bus drivers also provide commentary for one-day trips. Most localities have requirements for step-on guides that usually include obtaining a license by passing a test. If you enjoy interacting with people, disseminating information, and varied settings, this can be an ideal job. In fact, guides often say about their career, "Where else can you get paid for talking all you want and telling people where to go?"

Many tour guides work as independent contractors for different tour companies. The work demands that tour guides be highly knowledgeable, especially that they are able to navigate around the area and have a great deal of familiarity with local restaurants. Tour guides occasionally need to enforce alcohol and tobacco regulations and act as a counselor or therapist. Always, they must be diplomatic in dealing with their clients, because their dealings reflect, either negatively or positively, on the company for which they work. A successful tour guide must be patient and able to organize well and lead a group. Ability to speak in front of a group is another essential.

Work for step-on guides is seasonal, while tour escorts with packaged tours work year-round. You can also specialize in a certain market, such as planning international tours for a choir that include performances while on tour.

This work can be quite demanding, since it involves working seven days a week for many consecutive weeks, lifting luggage, and trying hard to keep all tour members happy. While not essential, knowledge of one or more foreign languages is a distinct asset. At the end of the century, the languages that are most helpful for tour guides in the United States are Spanish, Japanese, Russian, and German. A knowledge of art, history, and archaeology is also helpful. Tour guides must be able to think on their feet and deal with crises or unexpected changes that may occur, such as bus breakdowns or airline strikes. They must also enjoy learning about an area and communicating that information to tour members.

Degrees in tourism are available at some colleges, and some large tour companies provide training. However, most tour escorts learn their skills on the job, often working with seasoned escorts to learn about tour destinations and company policies. Some people arrive at escort and guide positions through contacts gained while working in other segments of the travel industry, such as a hotel or with an airline. Others obtain jobs by sending resumes to travel companies or tour operators whose destinations attract them.

The outlook for tour escorts and step-on guides is good, although the amount of expansion in the travel industry is directly related to the economy. When the economy is booming, people are willing to spend money on trips, and the field expands; the opposite occurs during recessions. At the end of the 1990s the travel industry was booming and only an economic downturn could change a positive outlook for this business.

See Profile, page 150.

RESOURCES

Camping

American Camping Association
5000 State Road 67 North
Martinsville, IN 46151-7902
Telephone: 317-342-8456
Fax: 317-3342-2065
Web: http://www.acacamps.org/

Canadian Camping Association
1810 Avenue Road, Suite 303
Toronto, Ontario M5M 3Z2
Telephone: 416-781-4717
Fax: 416-781-7875
Web:http://www.kidscamps.com/canadiancamping/index.htmlv

Diving Instruction
PADI
1251 East Cyer Road, #100
Santa Ana, CA 92705
Telephone: 714-540-7234 or 1-800-729-7234
Fax: 714-540-2690
Web: http://www.padi.com

NAUI Headquarters
P.O. Box 14650
Montclair, CA 91763
Telephone: 1-800-553-6284
Web: http://www.maui.org

Recreation and Cruise Ship Information
National Recreation and Park Association
22377 Belmont Ridge Road
Ashburn, VA 20148
Telephone: 703-858-0784
Fax: 703-671-6772
Web: http://www.nrpa.org/

Canadian Parks and Recreation Association
306-1600 James Naismith Drive
Gloucester, Ontario K1B 5N4
Telephone: 613-748-5651
Fax: 613-748-5854
Web: http://www.activeliving.ca/activeliving/cpra.html

American Association for Leisure and Recreation
1900 Association Drive
Reston, VA 22091
Telephone: 703-476-3472 or 1-800-213-7193
Web: http://www.aahperd.org/index.htm

The American Swimming Coaches Association
2101 North Andrews Avenue, Suite 107
Fort Lauderdale, FL 33311
Telephone: 954-563-4930 or 1-800-356-2722
Fax: 954-563-9813
Web: http://lornet.com/asca/

The Horse Industry

American Youth Horse Council
4093 Iron Works Pike
Lexington, KY 40511
Telephone: 1-800-879-2942
Fax: 606-299-9849

Professional Rodeo Cowboys Association
101 Pro Rodeo Drive
Colorado Springs, CO 80919-2301
Telephone: 719-593-8840
Fax: 719-548-4876
Web: http://www.sanctum.com/rodeo/prca.htm

Outfitters and Guides

Montana Outfitters & Guides Association
Box 1248
Helena, MT 59624
Telephone: 406-449-3578
Fax: 406-443-2439

Ski Patrolling

National Ski Patrol System
Ski Patrol Building, Suite 100
133 South Van Gordon
Lakewood, CO 80228
Telephone: 303-988-1111
Fax: 303-988-3005
Web: http://www.nsp.org/

Skydiving Instruction

United States Parachute Association
1440 Duke Street
Alexandria, VA 22314
Telephone: 703-836-3495
Fax: 703-836-2843
Web: http://www.uspa.org

Tourism

Travel Industry Association of America
1100 New York Avenue, NW, Suite 450
Washington, DC 20005
Telephone: 202-408-8422
Fax: 202-408-1255
Web: http://www.tia.org/default.asp

Web Sites

Cool Works—this large clearinghouse includes information
about recreation careers with jobs for cruise ships, private
resorts, ski areas, summer camps, and ranches
(http://www.coolworks.com/showme/)

Profile

EQUESTRIENNE
Phyllis Dawson

"The first word I ever said was *horse*. All I ever wanted to do was ride," says
Phyllis Dawson, a riding instructor and three-day event competitor who also
trains and boards horses at Windchase Farm near Hillsboro, Virginia.

Although Dawson grew up on a farm and began to teach riding and
board horses when she was in high school, she served an apprenticeship to
really learn the business. "I was a working student with a top-level competitor," she explains. "In this situation I was totally immersed in the stable and the day-to-day business."

While Dawson says college courses in horsemanship can be a place to
start for individuals who have no experience with horses, students do not
learn enough from this study to start in the business. "In the horse business

experience is very, very, very important," she emphasizes. "Also very important is your reputation for dealing honestly and giving your horses good care."

Dawson begins riding around 8:30 or 9 a.m. each day (although the stable is open earlier); she often starts earlier in the summer to avoid the heat. From 4 p.m. to 7 p.m. she gives riding lessons. "I ride my own high-level competition horses first and then I school the young horses I am training," she explains. "I now have students training with me who do some riding and help with the daily care and mucking stalls. But it has taken a long time to get this reputation.

"Working with horses involves long hours, few days off, low pay, and a lot of hard work. If you really love it, it's a great job—I wouldn't trade it for anything! Some people say to me, 'It must be wonderful to ride horses all day and not have a real job.' They don't understand."

During the event seasons (March to June and the end of August through early November) she enters competitions that test the same horse and rider in different events over three days. The first day is spent on dressage, a series of movements that tests the obedience, suppleness, finesse, and paces of the horse. Dawson compares dressage to the compulsory figures that used to be required in figure-skating competitions. The cross-country course, which is fifteen to eighteen miles long in the upper levels of competition that Dawson rides, is the most important of the events and tests the speed, endurance, boldness, and jumping ability of the horse. The third day of stadium jumping tests the horse's obedience and suppleness, as well as the conditioning that enables it to work the day after the long cross-country competition. The winner of the event is the horse-and-rider pair with the highest cumulative score from all three days.

"If I didn't compete I could take some time off, but competition is what attracts people to train with you," Dawson says. "And to coach you must stay current and in the upper levels of competition. It's all a part of the business." Dawson enjoys coaching, gaining satisfaction from watching her students progress. Additionally, she says that teaching helps her own riding improve.

People who enter this career must really want to do it, Dawson emphasizes. They must be very dedicated, love being outdoors, and love horses and working with them. The career also requires a long-term commitment. "To be in this career you must be able to come back after failures, disappointments, and the loss of a beloved horse. I have heard people say, 'If I don't make it to the top in a year or two I can always change careers.' Let me tell you, you don't make it to the top in a year or two!"

People in the horse business must also be able to relate well to other people, because boarding and training horses as well as teaching riding are all client based.

Dawson's work goes on in weather extremes from bitter cold to the heat of summer. Even her indoor arena is not heated or air conditioned. Nevertheless, Dawson says emphatically, "I like almost everything about it! I am totally happy doing what I am doing!" Even winning a lottery would change little about her schedule or work, she says, although she might buy a new truck and wouldn't feel pressured to keep every stall filled.

"There will always be a need for people in horse careers," Dawson declares. "It is a popular sport, so good instructors and trainers will always be in demand. Persons interested in this career must know that you do not get in it for the money. You must do it for the love of horses, of riding, and of training. It would be a terrible career if you didn't really love it."

Dawson's most exciting moment to date has been riding in the 1988 Summer Olympics in Seoul, Korea. To qualify for the U.S. team she went through selection trials that spring. At the Olympics she finished tenth in the individual three-day event, making her the highest-placed American. "Riding into that arena and seeing my name in lights with U.S.A. after it was the thrill of a lifetime!"

See The Horse Industry, page 137.

Profile
SKI PATROLLER
Michael Commins

"I spend virtually all my time outdoors—sometimes in the worst weather imaginable," says ski patroller Michael Commins. A California native, Commins learned to ski as a child, but says he entered this career by chance. "A friend got a job on a ski patrol in Sun Valley [Idaho] and I decided to try it also," he relates. More than twenty years later he still works in ski patrolling, now as a supervisor at the Grand Targhee Resort in Wyoming.

Ski patrollers promote safe skiing to the public through their contact with skiers and by posting temporary or permanent warning signs. They also give first aid to injured skiers. This includes everything from treating minor injuries to transporting badly injured skiers off the mountain on a toboggan.

"During the day we ski down the slopes about once an hour looking for problems or accidents," Commins explains. "At the end of the day we do the final run, called a sweep, to be certain that everyone is off the slopes. We make a visual check and stop often, listening for calls for help and calling out 'Sweep' or 'Final' to warn skiers to get off the slopes."

As ski patrol director, Commins has the additional responsibilities of recruiting, training, and supervising the ski patrollers. He suggests that individuals looking for patrolling jobs apply early, because applications often arrive a year in advance.

Commins says that the skills required for the job include proficiency in skiing and basic first-aid training. The National Ski Patrol's course in winter emergency care is essential. General outdoor experience in camping and hiking, such as that gained through Boy and Girl Scouts, is also helpful.

It may be easier for a beginning patroller to get a job at a small ski area than at a large one, Commins says; a move to a larger resort will be facilitated by experience. Although the pay is lower at smaller ski areas than at larger ones, smaller operations offer a more low-key environment for those who prefer such a setting.

College is not necessary for this career, but Commins suggests that it can help for advancement or as something to fall back on in case of injuries. Commins studied journalism with a minor in art, and although he did not obtain a degree, he has put his journalism studies to good use—his first book, Ski Patroller, was published in 1990, and he has written numerous articles for Ski Patrol magazine, the official publication of the National Ski Patrol.

The ski season runs from mid-November to the third week in April. Those who work as patrollers year after year (and many do, says Commins) work on summer jobs such as construction work (the season begins just as the ski slopes are closing), river-raft guiding, fishing guiding, or as tennis or golf pros.

For twelve years Commins drove trucks on highway construction crews during the off season, but for the last few years he has been fortunate enough to work at Grand Targhee year-round on ski-related work. During the off season Commins does small construction projects such as carpentry and electrical work. One summer he supervised a major landscaping project. To improve the ski trails, he trims trees and blasts rocks.

Commins is enthusiastic about his job: "I like the skiing time, working outdoors, helping others, and making a safer skiing environment. I like the camaraderie of working with a group of people who all like their jobs and work well together. This is mostly a low-pressure job, except when there are injuries."

Like most jobs, ski patrolling does have some negative aspects. The major one that Commins cites is dealing with people who break the rules. Some ski too fast, endangering themselves and others, while others want to ski in areas that are closed to the public—a misdemeanor in Wyoming.

Skiers often have knee problems. Commins has had operations on both knees and knows all too well what knee pain is like. Before and during the season he rides an indoor bicycle to keep his knees in shape.

Although pay is improving, ski patrollers do not receive high wages; supervisors do receive better pay. "Ski patrollers have to balance the money they earn," says Commins. "Generally, they earn more in their summer jobs."

People who seek out this career should be able to work well as part of a team and like to help others, according to Commins. Good verbal communications skills are essential, and the ability to do "nuts-and-bolts work" is helpful. Patrollers must also be able to handle the stress when injuries occur and make decisions quickly in a crisis. Commins says that the outlook for work in ski patrolling is good; there are openings every year.

See Ski Patrolling, page 139.

Profile

TOUR-BOAT CAPTAIN
Tim Jones

How did it happen that Tim Jones, with a bachelor's degree in journalism and years of experience on newspapers including the *Chicago Tribune* and the *Wall Street Journal*, became a tour-boat captain in Alaska?

It all started when Jones took a vacation in Alaska in 1973. He fell in love with the area. "It was the romance and the frontier aspect of the wild country that drew me," Jones says enthusiastically. As luck would have it, he was offered a job in Alaska on that same trip.

And so he moved to the state, working in Anchorage for seven years, first as news editor of the *Anchorage Daily News* and then with *Alaska* magazine. But he still wasn't where he wanted to be, and a boat trip to Prince William Sound set his course. "We have this humorous saying that 'Anchorage is the closest big city to Alaska,'" Jones laughs. "I absolutely fell in love with Prince William Sound. It has everything—mountains, ocean, glacier—and you could explore it for years."

Jones also fell in love with boating. Within a year he had his own boat, which he used for exploring the sound. Building on sailing knowledge from his youth, Jones learned how to navigate this boat by reading about the subject and practicing. But this still wasn't enough, so he began to save money so he could cut loose from his life in the city.

In early 1980 he achieved his goal. He quit his writing job, moved to a cabin he had built seven miles from the nearest road, and wrote a book. By summer he had obtained a small captain's license—"By that time I had enough time driving a boat to qualify for a Coast Guard license," he comments—and started working driving boats.

"It didn't pay much money," Jones admits, "and I had to get jobs in the winter to make ends meet." Nevertheless, he was able to live very simply in his cabin. "It was wonderful for me. But not everybody is cut out to live that way."

Two years later Jones began working for a larger company, and by 1984 he became captain of a tour boat. He was actually a jack-of-all-trades on the boat, functioning also as chief engineer and tour guide. "My wide range of interests helped me in working up the tour guide narration," he explains. "I did my own research and prepared the narration." It was a life that Jones enjoyed.

"It's really something to be a part of the boat world as a professional," he says enthusiastically. "The camaraderie among the people who work in the harbor is just great." He also enjoyed the trips. "Every trip was different. You saw different species of wildlife on each trip."

The job had its downside, however. The greatest drawback for Jones was the fact that the tour boat was confined to a specific route during the tour, and he "couldn't get to other and exciting parts of the sound." Also, being a jack-of-all-trades had its tedious aspects. "There was a lot of maintenance in taking care of a large boat that has to meet Coast Guard specifications and has to run all the time," Jones confides. "Some people also got really tired by the end of the season. One summer I worked for 120 days without any time off."

For anyone who aspires to this type of life, Jones advises realistically, "It's important to be prepared not to make a lot of money. The tourist trade is very seasonal, and in Alaska summer is a short season. To make ends meet you need to either live simply in the off seasons or take a job.

"I adopted a philosophy I call 'creative poverty.' I didn't take any job that had no specific ending time, and I saved half of the money I earned. Thus for every day I worked I knew I was buying a day of freedom."

During the winters Jones wrote. He has written three books. The first two are about the Iditarod, the Alaska sled-dog race from Anchorage to Nome. The first is a general look at the race, and the second was cowritten with the first female Iditarod winner. His third book is a departure, a book of nursery rhymes written to accompany high-quality photographs of Alaska taken by a friend. He also managed a local paper, the *Nome Nugget*, during one off season.

Jones's goal was to enjoy life and have time to do what he wanted to do: write. The Exxon *Valdez* spill temporarily ended this life for Jones. He had an accident while assisting with the cleanup and left the tour-boat life.

"This oil spill has ruined Prince William Sound for me and many other Alaskans," Jones explains. "Between the oil fouling the sound and the many people who came in for the cleanup [which he says has not been effective], the sound has changed." Although he still loves the sound, it doesn't draw him as it used to.

Jones now works for a salmon hatchery in the sound as fishing vessel administrator. His major responsibility is to coordinate a program that would use local fishing boats to assist in the event of another oil spill. "I like the fact that this job would allow me to make something happen if there were another oil spill," he says.

Jones speaks of his tour-boat days nostalgically and says he and his wife are planning to return to a life like that someday.

See The Tourism Industry, page 142.

Chapter 9

Indoor Careers with
an Outdoor Twist

*For me the preservation and celebration of the natural world is
a continual concern and the underlying motive for virtually
all of my art.*

Robert Bateman

Many people who passionately love the outdoors find satisfaction in
careers that are largely spent indoors but have the outdoors as their
vital ingredient. Indoor skills are required for these types of work, but they
build upon knowledge of the outdoors as well as a love of the outdoors
and outdoor life.

Artists who concentrate on nature and wildlife subjects spend their
working time inside while focusing on the outdoors; they also spend
research time outside. Nature photographers spend a great deal of time outside taking pictures, but they also spend a fair amount of time indoors planning their trips, making the necessary contacts, and performing other tasks
that are an essential part of their work. Teachers who teach subjects related
to the outdoors—such as geography, environmental sciences, or agronomy—often do outside research in preparation for or as part of their work.

Writing and editing also mainly involve working inside but may spot-
light outdoor topics. Here, a keen knowledge of the outdoors is required,
as is the ability to conduct research. In fact, writing can be combined with
another career that is not full time or year-round, such as recreation, to provide a full-time living for an outdoor enthusiast.

Organizations that focus on preserving and maintaining the natural
world offer many types of positions. Often these indoor jobs require some
knowledge of, and dedication to, the outdoors. Some companies are also

adding the function of environmental accountant to their staff. This person works to save money for the company while incorporating environmentally sound practices.

Owners and workers in stores that supply outdoor equipment, from camping and hiking to scuba diving, also fall into this category. For these people, their interest in and expertise about the outdoors, however narrowly focused, adds to the knowledge they bring to their work and the enjoyment they derive from it.

This chapter concentrates on several careers that require specific skills. Don't let this limit you; rather, use it as a point from which to take off. Use these examples, other possibilities, or your own creativity to find your own niche.

For example, you may have artistic talent and interest in becoming an artist. If you don't succeed in making a career as an artist, however—perhaps because of timing, market volatility, or location—you might become involved in gallery management or work as an agent for a painter or group of painters. Here, knowledge of the field would be a distinct advantage, and you will be able to work in an arena of particular interest to you.

You may have to put together several options to find the work best suited to your own unique mix of skills, interests, and aptitudes. But when you do, the result will be happiness in work that you have chosen.

WILDLIFE AND NATURE ART

Salary Range	Quite varied and unpredictable
Educational Requirements	Art courses are an asset
Employment Outlook	In stable economic times, good for artists with clientele

Wildlife and nature art has almost become a field in itself; unfortunately, however, some art galleries do not consider it a real art. Still, it has blossomed in the twentieth century with the work of such pioneers as John James Audubon and Roger Tory Peterson, who focused exclusively on birds in their paintings. As more people have become interested in art depicting the outdoors and outdoor creatures, the market for wildlife and nature art has grown, and so has the number of artists who can make a living from it.

In this art field the approach to the work is as different as each individual artist. For example, most wildlife artists prefer to work from their own experience in the field. This means trips to the wild lugging equipment such as cameras and sketchpads. It may also mean long days in the outdoors looking for subjects and frantic moments of photography or sketching before the elusive subject melts away into the wild. Others may use zoos or wildlife preserves, which do not require such an arduous approach to locating the subject matter.

If you love the outdoors, some of the career satisfaction comes from being outside doing the research. Completion of a work to your own standards is another reward. And if your works become sought after and command high prices ($5,000 and up per piece), another satisfaction comes from the money earned.

To succeed in this career, an obvious requirement is that you be artistically gifted. Without this innate gift, no amount of study and work will enable you to produce artistic creations that large numbers of people are willing to buy. Artistic gifts are, however, subjective; what appeals to one individual may be quite unattractive to another. So it's important that you believe in your own ability or artistic potential. Other essential traits for an artist are imagination and creativity, persistence, patience (especially when working in the field), determination, independence, and sensitivity.

Most successful wildlife and nature artists have studied art, and many have studied biology or zoology in college. These courses complement artistic ability with knowledge of animals and birds and their habitats.

Artists frequently enter this field from a full-time job in another, often related, career. This allows them time to develop both their artistic skills and a market for their work. Others may continue to augment their art income with full- or part-time work. Some complementary jobs are those of art teacher, art director, graphic designer, or teaching in your own studio.

Painting—with acrylics, oils, or watercolors—is probably the most common form of art used by nature and wildlife artists. Photography is another major form of art dealing with the outdoors. This varied art field, however, also includes ink drawing, illustration, sculpture, carving, and what are often called crafts, such as decorating napkin holders with bird paintings or notepaper with a batik wildlife illustration.

See Profiles, pages 165 and 168.

TEACHING

Salary Range	For university and college teachers, this depends on the institution; instructors average $30,000, assistant professors $39,200, associate professors $45,800, and full professors $64,000. For secondary school teachers the average starting salary is about $22,000, median $37,000, and top $42,000. All teaching salaries vary depending on the location and educational background of the teacher; secondary salaries are especially affected by location.
Educational Requirements	For university and college, doctorate or completion in progress. For secondary schools, a bachelor's degree plus additional training is minimal, a master's desirable.
Employment Outlook	For university and college teaching—average or slower. For secondary school teachers—higher than average, especially in the southern and western United States (where the population is growing rapidly) and in inner city and rural areas (which do not attract many teachers).

Universities and Colleges

Teaching offers a good opportunity to deal with outdoor-related subjects from an indoor location. And for many teaching positions at the university level, an essential component is research, which often involves work in the outdoors. Teachers of many subjects, such as plant pathology, need to continue research to maintain current knowledge in their field.

Teachers also need to read current literature and attend conferences to learn what others in the field are doing. Writing their research findings in scholarly journals is essential for college and university faculty members; such writing is usually considered in the decision of whether they receive tenure, or job security.

At the university or college level, teachers need to prepare lectures, laboratory experiments, and exercises; grade exams and papers; and work one on one with students as necessary. They may lecture in large halls to classes numbering in the hundreds, conduct seminars of smaller groups of students, direct laboratory periods, or supervise graduate students in teaching, research, and experiments.

Faculty members usually teach several courses in their department. They are often involved with academic committees relating to the policies of the institution. The amount of time spent on each of these activities will depend on the institution and the individual faculty member.

College teachers generally have flexible schedules. Aside from being available for their classes and institutional meetings, they can organize their time as desired. Depending on their teaching schedule, they may have time off during the summer for research, travel, or personal interests.

Teaching can be intellectually challenging and stimulating, and the flexibility it offers can be very attractive. With tight budgets and possibly declining enrollment, institutions of higher learning are hiring more faculty members on a part-time basis than previously. Many of these part-time personnel also have jobs outside the institution or balance part-time positions in more than one institution. Part-time faculty members usually do not have benefits as part of their contracts, however—a definite negative. But a part-time job may eventually lead to a full-time job. It may also be the answer if you want to spend more working time outside, as long as you locate the right part-time job to complement a part-time faculty position.

The competition for faculty positions at universities and colleges has become strong as budgets have been cut. Many teachers have accepted, instead, part-time or short-term positions. There are some indications that this may change, because the number of students is expected to rise. Additionally, some academic fields may be expanding because of current problems, such as environmental degradation and waste disposal.

Tenure is a permanent contract for which faculty members qualify after having worked for a certain period of time, usually seven years. At the university level, a doctorate is required for tenure; also, tenure is granted only if your teaching, research, and general contribution to the university are favorable and if tenured positions are available. You may be hired while completion of your doctorate is still in progress, but completion within a certain time limit is essential.

Obtaining a doctorate is usually a matter of four to seven years of full-time study after a bachelor's degree. A dissertation, a major paper reporting on research conducted in an important area of study in the field, must also be completed.

Teaching positions in some university departments—such as art, dance, and law—may require certain qualifications other than a doctorate.

Important qualifications for college and university teaching are intelligence, a mind that questions and analyzes information, and a love of knowledge. Verbal and written communications skills are essential, as is the ability to establish rapport with students. Ability to work without direct supervision is also essential.

Secondary Schools

Secondary school teachers educate students from grades seven through twelve (in some districts this may be grades five through twelve). They are responsible for teaching certain subjects—either academic classes or skill-demanding courses such as art or woodworking—supervising extracurricular activities, and serving on committees. Secondary school teaching involves team planning with other teachers, administrators, school counselors, and psychologists. Some involvement with parents and parent groups as well as the community is also important.

Secondary school teachers must have a good knowledge of the subject or subjects they teach and the ability to communicate that information. Being able to relate well to students and to motivate them to study are other important qualities.

Generally, secondary school teachers teach from four to seven classes a day. They may also be in charge of a homeroom, where they take attendance, or study halls, where they maintain a quiet atmosphere conducive to study.

Teaching secondary school students—helping educate the youth of a country at the beginning of the twenty-first century—is a challenging and rewarding career. It requires spending evenings and weekends in class preparation and grading tests and assignments. Troubles facing many schools—such as drugs, disciplinary problems, and violence against teachers and other students—can make secondary school teaching more difficult.

Each state or province has specific certification requirements for secondary school teachers. These vary from government to government, but generally to obtain certification you must have a bachelor's degree in your subject. Teaching experience and classes in education are usually required; these may be included in the bachelor's degree or taken in a year of study after earning a bachelor's. Increasingly, a master's degree or study toward one is becoming important for secondary school teachers. Written or oral exams may also be required. It is important to check the requirements, as well as projected needs, for secondary school teachers in the state or province where you wish to teach before you embark upon this career.

Secondary school teachers usually teach classes that range from ten to thirty students in size. They must be able to spend most of the day standing and to speak for a great deal of that time. Teaching hours are generally between 9 a.m. and 3 p.m., but this will vary with location. Summer months are usually free; many teachers use this time for additional study or to earn extra income. Some teachers use the summer for outdoor work to balance their regular indoor work.

WRITING AND EDITING

Salary Range	Depends on location, employer, and work; beginning about $16,000, averaging about $25,000, and topping off at $70,000-plus; technical writing is most remunerative; freelance writing and editing pay depends on the organization and the name recognition of the writer
Educational Requirements	College usually expected, but demonstrated ability is most important
Employment Outlook	Good

The work of writers and editors centers on written communication. Writers produce magazine and newspaper articles, books, newsletters, and radio and television scripts. Editors organize publications, supervise or contact writers, and prepare material for publication or broadcast. As communication through the World Wide Web expands, producing Internet copy—for example, for the Web pages of outdoor organizations—will also become increasingly important for writers and editors.

Writing and editing related to the outdoors offer many career possibilities. You might write and edit as the major focus of your career, or combine these activities with a seasonal outdoor career to provide an adequate-to-good living. If you're skilled and interested in the outdoors, you'll bring an additional dimension to writing and editing material about this subject that cannot be matched by those simply working on assignment.

Writers gather information through personal observation and experience, research, and interviews. They then attempt to find the best words to convey this information to the reader. For most writers, revising and rewriting are essential in the process of communicating information.

Writers may work on a freelance basis, although this is easiest for established writers to do. Others may be employed full time by a particular publication, organization, or company.

While many editors do some writing in addition to rewriting and editing, their major focus is the overall content of a publication or a radio or television production. For printed materials, editors may select and assign topics and oversee the production process. For radio or television productions, the editorial function is geared more strictly to the content, and production managers take over the final stages.

Editors may have a number of assistants to help in the publication process. These may include copy editors, who check for errors in grammar, punctuation, and spelling; assistant editors, who edit copy for style, agreement with editorial policy, and readability, and may also do some rewriting; and editorial assistants, who may assist writers by doing research and verifying facts.

For freelance work, the necessary requirement is a demonstrated ability to write or edit well. Degrees or education are definite assets, but the proof of ability is in the actual work produced. For part- or full-time positions with an organization or on a publication, the requirement is usually a college degree; some employers prefer English, journalism, or communications graduates, while others prefer a broad liberal arts background.

Writing and editing are specific skills that require clear and logical expression. Valuable traits for writers include creativity, perseverance, and self-motivation. A wide range of knowledge and intellectual curiosity are also important. Familiarity with word processing is almost essential, and computer publishing knowledge is helpful. Practical writing experience—through high school or college papers, volunteer work, an internship, or freelance work—is very important in this field.

Editors also usually need a knowledge of desktop publishing. For many positions, the judgment and ability to select material for publication and to organize are essential as well. Tact in dealing with others and the ability to advise and assist others in their work are other important qualities for editors.

Although the demand for writers and editors is expected to remain strong, competition for jobs and for freelance work will remain intense because many people are attracted to this field. Breaking into the field is especially difficult for beginners; students are often advised to prepare for another occupation and try to enter through freelance work. The main factor in getting jobs here is a demonstrated proof of ability. Those who want very badly to be writers or editors and have the skills will usually find a way. The need for books will continue, even in this TV and Internet age. A demand for TV, radio, and Internet scripts will also fuel positions. Much of this work will go to freelance writers.

Writing and editing jobs can be excellent forums for those concerned about issues of conservation and preservation of natural resources.

See Profile, page 170.

CONSERVATION AND ENVIRONMENTAL ORGANIZATION WORK

Salary Range	Extremely varied, depending on the size of the organization, location, and position; from about $20,000 for clerical workers to $150,000-plus for executive directors
Educational Requirements	From high school diploma to doctorate, depending on the position
Employment Outlook	Good, although a recession will cause organizations to tighten their belts

Many associations and organizations center on conservation, the environment, and other issues related to the outdoors. These organizations have varied types of positions, and they offer a good platform for outdoor concerns. These associations come in all sizes; the types and scope of positions at each organization directly relate to its size and purpose.

Members of these organizations have a common interest or background in a certain subject or profession such as wildlife, the environment, or conservation. Members join because of interest or to increase their expertise. Average staff size is from ten to thirty employees, although some large organizations have more than a thousand staff members, with very specialized functions.

Keeping members informed is a major function of all of these associations. Many also work to influence policy or events. The various tasks association staffers may perform include writing special studies; publishing magazines, books, newspapers, or news releases; giving public speeches or lobbying on special issues; arranging meetings, seminars, and conventions; handling marketing and sales functions; and arranging shows and exhibitions.

Association positions include executive director, writers and editors, legislative staff members or lobbyists, public relations personnel, researchers, and fund-raisers.

The Nature Conservancy is an example of a large organization with varied career positions available around the United States and abroad. A commitment to conservation is important for all jobs with this organization, whose major purpose is to preserve natural diversity. The Conservancy does this by identifying, protecting, and managing the lands and waters that imperiled species of plants, birds, and mammals need to survive.

Through its focus on preserving biodiversity, the Conservancy sets clear priorities and targets resources accordingly. Its science-based, nonconfrontational approach has given The Nature Conservancy the ability to work with a broad array of partners and to develop innovative conservation strategies.

In the United States the Conservancy has protected more than ten million acres of ecologically important habitat, and it owns and manages more than fourteen hundred preserves—the largest system of private nature preserves in the world. In Latin America, the Caribbean, Asia, and the Pacific, the Conservancy works in partnership with local conservation groups and government agencies helping to protect more than fifty-five million acres.

The corporate headquarters is in metropolitan Washington, D.C., but only about four hundred staffers work there. The rest work on nature preserves or in local, state, regional, or international offices.

Full-time positions in the Conservancy fall into eight categories: science and stewardship, or preserve management; legal; international; fundraising and communications; government relations; data systems, accounting, and finance; management and administration; and administrative and secretarial support. The Conservancy also has part-time, seasonal, internship, and volunteer positions. A national employment hotline (703-247-3721) is updated every week with job vacancies, including fulltime and intern positions. Regional and state Conservancy offices also have employment information.

The United States, Canada, and the United Kingdom all have many different associations and organizations. The largest single grouping of national and international organizations in the United States is in the Washington, D.C., area. Similarly, Ottawa in Canada and London in England have a large number of organizational offices. For organizations with a great need to contact the country's government, locating in or near the capital city is a real asset. In the United States other top locations are Boston and New York City, but associations can be found all around the

Museum Work

American Association of Museums
Technical Information Service
1575 Eye Street, NW, Suite 400
Washington, DC 20005
Telephone: 202-289-1818
Fax: 202-289-6578
Web: http://www.aam-us.org/

For museum interships and fellowships:
Center for Museum Studies
900 Jefferson Drive SW
Room 2235, MRC 427
Smithsonian Institution
Washington, DC 20560
Telephone: 202-357-3101
Web: http://www.si.edu./cms

Canadian Museums Association
280 Metcalfe Street, Suite 400
Ottawa, Ontario K2P 1R7
Telephone: 613-567-0099
Fax: 613-233-5438
Web: http://www.museums.ca/home.htm

Canadian Heritage Information Network
Web: http://www.chin.gc.ca/e_main_menu.html)

Profile

NATURE ARTIST
Robert Bateman

"My goal in life has always been to live in or near nature. Supporting myself with my art was never a goal," confides internationally known artist Robert Bateman, who describes himself as "an artist who's interested in nature."

Bateman's basis for this quality of life was teaching; he taught high school art and geography for twenty years before becoming a full-time painter. He enjoyed teaching. "I couldn't see why they paid me all that money to have fun talking to a bunch of teenagers," Bateman admits. "I would come home from teaching and get on with my life: doing art and having adventures in nature."

This Canadian artist has garnered an international reputation for realism in portraying animals and nature. In some of his paintings the wildlife subject almost appears to be leaving the canvas, or is hard to locate. The care Bateman gives to the natural settings in his painting reveals his passionate love of nature. His concern for the natural world is also shown in his involvement in international and local environmental causes. Bateman gives about five to ten speeches a year—speeches that he characterizes as "getting more and more militantly environmental." This involvement recently earned him two prestigious awards: the Rachel Carson Award, presented by the Society of Environmental Toxicologists and Chemists in 1996, and the Golden Plate Award from the American Academy of Achievement in 1998.

Bateman does not take himself or his success too seriously. In fact, this personable and outgoing artist has a problem with the word *success*. "To me," he says matter-of-factly, "success is how well I do each painting and how I'm thought of by my peers and people whose opinions I respect."

Bateman's love of nature began in his youth and was nurtured through family interests, naturalist clubs, and summers working on wildlife research or geological field parties. He has a bachelor's degree in geography and a high school teaching certificate. Early in his teaching career, he traveled around the world in a Land Rover while he and a naturalist friend collected specimens for the Royal Ontario Museum. These travels and the two years he spent teaching geography in Africa have influenced his paintings.

Patience is the first quality Bateman cites as important for artists. Also important, he adds, is "the ability to really look, not just superficially glance, at something." Perhaps the most important trait, however, is one he often finds lacking in budding artists. "It is important to be a tough and observant critic of the project you're working on. I'm just amazed at the things young artists don't notice about their own work.

"I would advise aspiring artists to get a meal ticket so they don't have to paint for the market," Bateman continues. "It's dangerous to start selling too young; artists may start imitating themselves instead of going on to find their own artistic voice. Art is a unique and special individual expression. Artists who paint for the market too early may put a ceiling on their creativity and never rise above mediocrity.

"I have a specific routine when I'm painting," he explains. "I work from nine o'clock in the morning until noon. I take a walk before lunch, and after lunch I have a nap and coffee before I get back to painting. I have another walk before dinner. When the weather's nice, I eat outside. I often paint in the evening." The painting routine gives him one or two hours a day outdoors, although he has a magnificent view of nature from his studio window. His research is done in the field, concentrating on habitat and the effect of light and atmosphere on landscapes large and small.

On book tours Bateman's schedule consists of an early start for a radio or TV interview, a newspaper interview, catching the noon crowds at a bookstore, another newspaper interview after lunch, catching the evening crowds in a bookstore over the dinner hour, and then either a lecture or traveling on to the next town in the evening. His fourth book, *Robert Bateman: Natural Worlds*, was published in 1996, and *Safari*, a book for children featuring his paintings of African animals, was published in 1998.

About the business end of painting, Bateman says, "Luckily, I have never had to go out and sell. I have no talent or interest in that direction." His first show in 1967 sold out on opening night, and the demand for his art has remained constant ever since. He is regularly inundated with requests for his participation in environmental or artistic endeavors; indeed, he now has two full-time assistants to handle the demand.

Bateman's actual work as an artist has not been affected by the new technology. Having a fax machine and e-mail has, however, increased the efficiency of communication. His Web site (http://www.batemanideas.com) deals, however, with Bateman's ideas, not his art. The site leads off with this Schumacher quote: "The real problems facing this planet are not economic or technical, they are philosophical." The site also includes links to talks or writings by Bateman that give an indication of the intellectual depth and focus of this artist. Only two of the fifteen links deal directly with art; the rest reveal Bateman's focus on changing approaches to solving today's problems. He quotes Albert Einstein's statement: "We cannot solve the problems of today with the same thinking that gave us those problems in the first place."

Bateman and his wife, Birgit, travel extensively. Bateman says of Birgit, "She is a true kindred spirit who is an integral part of my life and work." Birgit is herself an artist as well as an avid photographer and a naturalist. She is very involved in Robert's career—helping him plan shows, critiquing his work, and handling many business and charity matters.

Although his paintings hang in the private collections of the rich and famous around the world, Bateman remains modest and unpretentious. He remarks philosophically, "It may not continue. I remember reading this slogan: 'No condition is permanent.' . . . But the only problem if my paintings don't sell would be a bruise to my ego."

See Wildlife and Nature Art, page 154.

Profile

WILDLIFE PHOTOGRAPHER
Heather Angel

Becoming a wildlife photographer was not Heather Angel's intention when she attended university. Her major in zoology, however, was a natural progression from her love of wildlife and nature nurtured by vacations on her grandparents' farm in Suffolk, England, where she learned the names of wildflowers. She also collected insects as a youth: "My mother never knew what she might find in kitchen containers—live crayfish in a casserole or caterpillars in a jam jar," says Angel.

The event that redirected her energies occurred when, bored by a tedious research task in marine biology, she wrote an article about sea anemones accompanied by her own color photos. More articles followed; she wrote her first book, at her husband's suggestion, when she could not find a book on nature photography to recommend to others. "Overnight, this changed my life," Angel says. "Suddenly several photographic magazines asked me to write for them and the emphasis shifted from me being a biologist taking a few pictures to a nature photographer with a biological background.

"Wildlife photography," continues Angel, "involves working on location taking wildlife in its natural habitat. I traverse the globe, from the poles to the tropics, annually. This may involve trekking over rough terrain or sitting for hours in a blind and waiting either for animals to appear or [for] the perfect light. Potentially dangerous carnivores, such as polar bears, have to be worked from a vehicle specially designed for traversing the tundra, with tires six feet in diameter.

"Unlike many wildlife artists," she says, "I enjoy the selling side of my business. Some of my books arise as a result of a publisher approaching me, but there is nothing I love more than producing a visual presentation for a new book." Heather Angel's forty-six books are testimony to her success.

She divides her time among photographing, writing, and research. Most of her ideas for subjects come from field observations. "Ever since I started," she says, "I have only photographed what motivates me. I have accepted very few commissions." Her daily schedule on location "depends in which part of the world and which habitat I am working." She makes it a point, no matter where she is, to be in the field before dawn so she can catch evocative lighting. During downtimes (when animals don't appear, the weather is foul, or she must wait in airports), she makes notes about habitats, types of plants, behavior of animals that are not her current subject, and book ideas.

Angel says that a love of nature is more important than basic photographic knowledge for her career. "Also a keen eye and the ability to work in all weather," she adds, along with "knowledge about the habitat and habits of your subject. You need to know where to find subjects and when animals are courting, breeding, migrating, or whatever behavior you want to portray. Time spent researching a location can avoid wasting time in the field." Another crucial skill is "having a seeing eye to dissect a memorable image from the plethora of possible pictures." Finally, you'll need contacts; Angel has "a vast array of wardens, biologists, and photographers who help me out. In turn, I provide information for other photographers."

Essential personality traits for wildlife photographers, says Angel, are: "patience, patience, patience; dedication; ability to prioritize jobs; and always meeting client deadlines." Quick reflexes help in photographing wildlife on the move.

Among the things that Angel loves about her career are seeing wilderness areas, leaving the telephone and fax behind, and setting her own deadline on a shoot. She also enjoys seeing the films immediately after processing, "unless there has been a disaster with a camera!"

Downsides include the letters and telephone calls that accumulate while she is on a shoot, and the tedium of editing and captioning pictures. Additionally, freelance photographers must cover all their own expenses: film purchase, processing of original slides, making duplicates of the best frames, telephone, fax, Internet server rental, postage, printing, couriers, stationery, travel, advertising, gear insurance, vehicles, computer, filing cabinets, and hanging sheets for slides. Working in all types of weather and extreme temperatures—Angel has worked in –30 °C (–22 ° F) and to 40 ° C (104 ° F)—are other negatives.

If you're interested in working as a wildlife photographer, Angel suggests two career paths. One is to study biology at school, develop writing skills, and then work for a local paper while learning photography and field craft on the side. The second path is to study biology and take a course or degree in photography (with a focus on wildlife and nature) or in photojournalism. Still, while Angel calls wildlife photography "a great career for anyone who enjoys working outdoors and loves wildlife," she warns that it's highly competitive. Have a backup plan, she advises, and don't leave a regular job until you are certain that photography will pay.

Indeed, she says, only a few among the many would-be wildlife photographers make a good living. "Having another string to your bow certainly helps. Being able to write and produce complete text and picture packages is an advantage over trying to market individual images." Another strategy that Angel advises is an "in-depth study of a single charismatic species." She cites her specialty in pandas—both giant and red. "This has resulted in more magazine covers than any other animal I have photographed."

Although realistic about the downside of her career, Angel concludes that "anyone who is determined to succeed will get there if they produce quality and original work. I, for one, would never contemplate another job."

See Wildlife and Nature Art, page 154.

Profile

OUTDOOR WRITER AND TRAIL BUILDER
Bob Birkby

"I got interested in the outdoors through my father, leader of the local Scout troop, and hundreds of camp-outs in the corn," relates Bob Birkby, an Iowa native who now works as an outdoor writer and trail builder. The six summers he worked at Philmont—a Boy Scout camp in northern New Mexico—as a backcountry trail crew foreman and later as director of conservation added to his love of the outdoors. "In addition to being great fun," Birkby recalls, "those summers taught me the basics of wilderness leadership and also gave me a fair expertise in trail construction and maintenance."

Birkby earned bachelor's and master's degrees in English and spent three years teaching writing at Southwest Missouri State University. "I was well on the way to a lifetime as a college professor," Birkby says, "but there was a small matter of the Appalachian Trail. It was just, well, out there, demanding to be hiked. In fact, there was a whole lot of out there out there, and the confines of classrooms, libraries, and faculty meetings were bringing on major career claustrophobia."

So Birkby quit his teaching job, hiked the Appalachian Trail from Maine to Georgia, and headed west, arriving in Seattle about the time his savings ran out.

He first wrote a novel, but he decided it was not worthy of print. Then he began writing short articles about the odd jobs that had paid his rent. In search of another job, he came in contact with the Student Conservation

Association (SCA), which immediately offered him a job supervising a high school trail crew. "It was a perfect match for me—the chance to teach, to use my trail construction skills, and to spend extended periods in the backcountry," explains Birkby. "Over the years I've supervised SCA programs along the Buffalo River in Arkansas, in the Nez Perce National Forest in Idaho, at the bottom of the Grand Canyon, and in Yellowstone, Glacier, and Kings Canyon National Parks. In 1990 I directed the SCA exchange program with the Soviet Union, spending the first half of the summer in Yellowstone and the second half in the national parks of Latvia and Estonia."

Birkby is also an instructor in the SCA Wilderness Work Skills Program and a writer for the Boy Scouts of America. Using his contacts from previous work with the Boy Scouts, he got a job writing an eighty-page merit badge pamphlet under a very tight deadline, and, says Birkby, "The BSA and I were on our way." He has done other work for the Boy Scouts, including writing columns for *Boys' Life* magazine, revising camping and hiking merit badge pamphlets, and writing new editions of the *Boy Scout Handbook* and *Scoutmaster Handbook*. Along the way he has also written *Learn How to Canoe in One Day* and *Lightly on the Land: The SCA Trail-Building and Maintenance Manual*.

"When I left teaching, I had hopes of finding a career that involved writing and outdoor adventures, but I didn't have a clue where to begin finding it," Birkby confides. "Now I write six or seven months of the year, and then when the snow melts out of the mountains, I head for places high and wild. There have been years when my outdoor work in the summer has supported a winter of writing, and years when what I earn as a writer has funded my summer adventures.

"The world of outdoor writing has its own wicked difficulties. Over the years I've known lots of people who wanted to be/were becoming/were convinced they were outdoor writers. The older I get, though, the fewer people I know who are my age and still writing. It is a career with a brutal attrition rate.

"When asked if she enjoyed writing, Gertrude Stein said no, but she enjoyed having written. I think that is at the heart of outdoor writing careers—from the outside it sure seems like an exciting way to make a living (and in fact there are times when it is). The reality, though, is that it is a discipline just as demanding and harsh as mountaineering. To survive as a writer, you've got to have an innate love for how words fit together—you've got to like playing with the language. You also need to have something to write about, and that means getting in the field, seeing what there is to see, and developing some clear opinions. Hardest of all, you have to hunker down and just do it—sit at a desk and hammer out the work for days, weeks, and months at a time.

"There is no typical career path to becoming a writer/trail builder. Nor is there a typical day's work. Last week I got up, wrote until I couldn't see straight, went to bed; this week I flew to Latvia, built rustic hiking bridges, went to bed.

"Like a full-time mountaineer, a writer takes on the responsibility for inventing his own career. That can be extremely scary at times. For many people, the uncertainty is too much to deal with. But when the pieces fall in place and the adventures and the writing mesh into one glorious flow, there is no better way to live."

See Writing and Editing, page 159.

Chapter 10

Some Job-Search Tips

The greater the number of job-hunting avenues you use, the greater the likelihood that you will find a job.
Richard Nelson Bolles, *What Color Is Your Parachute?*

Now that you've reached this chapter you've probably focused on a specific career or career area. At this point it will be helpful to do some additional research before you begin your job search in earnest. Look at books and other resources that cover the particular career in greater detail. Especially valuable, if you have no work or volunteer experience in your chosen field, are informational interviews with people currently working in the field. This will help round out your knowledge of that career and will also give you contacts who may be helpful when you begin your job search.

This chapter explains how the Internet can help you, reviews some of the critical aspects of this part of the job-search process, and points the way to additional and more detailed information.

THE INTERNET

If you haven't already used the Internet in your search for career information, you may want to start now. If you're not familiar with it, get some assistance from local resources such as a library or career center. You might also consult the Resources section at the end of this chapter.

A cautionary note, however, before you spend any time using the Internet in your career search. As you may already know, it is easy to become engrossed in an Internet search, following links from one site to another. Before you begin each Internet session, decide how much time you will spend online and how much information you want to locate. This will help ensure that your time is well spent.

The Internet contains a wide variety of resources, whose usefulness varies as widely as do the books in a bookstore. Before you dip too deeply into any specific Web site, try to evaluate the site and its purpose. Use the same criteria you use when you open a printed book. Determine who established the site and why, and then decide how these factors might affect the validity of the information. Also try to find out when the information was posted; it will be most helpful to use the most current information in your search.

The Resources section of each chapter in this book contains the Web addresses of the various organizations listed, whenever available. This is a good place to begin, especially if you're not Web savvy. Many of these organizational Web sites contain career information and actual job listings, or links to sites that have this information. As you would expect, sites vary considerably in the type and amount of information they contain.

Some companies and organizations advertise jobs on the Internet and accept résumés for these jobs online. Governments throughout the United States, especially at the national and state levels, list available jobs. The Canadian national and provincial governments also list available jobs. Many universities and colleges list jobs on Web sites that are protected from use by individuals other than their own graduates. You should explore all assistance available from your own institution, while also checking other sources.

You may also decide to establish your own home page, complete with your résumé. Some individuals have found work using this method. Other Web sites allow you to post your résumé without charge. Additionally, some discussion groups on the Internet give job listings. Used wisely, the Internet can be a wonderful tool for finding a good job. In fact, recruiters are increasingly using the Internet. Of some forty-three hundred recruiters surveyed in 1998, 37 percent used the Web, a 10 percent increase from the year before.

If you wish to use the Internet extensively in your job search, be sure to check the Career Crossroads Web site (and other books and sites) in the Resources listing at the end of this chapter.

WRITING YOUR RÉSUMÉ

A résumé is an essential job-search tool, and preparing one is among the first steps to take in a job search. Remember that a résumé is a selective summary of your skills, abilities, work, and study experiences. It is not a life history, but it should provide enough critical information about your background to interest a potential employer in interviewing you.

Writing your résumé, instead of hiring a résumé service to prepare one for you, is a valuable part of the job-search process. Although résumé writing takes effort, it's well worth your time as well as excellent preparation for the focus on your background that will occur in the job interview. If you do consult an outside source for help, be sure that you are actively involved in the process.

In writing a résumé, be certain to include all of your applicable skills and experience to ensure that you are presenting yourself as favorably as possible. Because a résumé is usually the second representation of yourself to a potential employer (after your cover letter), it must be clear, concise, and well written. Before you begin to write the actual résumé, take some time to jot down information that you think should be included. Organize your information under the following headings.

Career Objective

Your career objective, a simple statement of the kind of career you are seeking, should also include brief information about your skills or background. Some people do not feel comfortable writing a career objective and prefer to give a skills summary. The value of this information, however, is that it helps focus your résumé and gives a potential employer a good overview of your background.

Skills and Work Experience

Write out your work experience and then elaborate, listing the skills you used in each job. It is important to describe what you actually did or accomplished. If you are a recent graduate or are changing careers, you can include summer, part-time, or volunteer positions as well as extracurricular activities. The focus here should not be on any job title, which can often be misleading, but on the job content. What actual skills did the job entail?

Your résumé should show the skills you have used and give examples of your accomplishments. In detailing your skills and accomplishments, use action verbs. The many résumé books available usually give comprehensive listings of such verbs.

If you are changing careers, remember that you may use some of the same skills in the new career that you used in previous work. For example, you may be moving from a supervisory position to an editing and writing position. Many supervisory positions involve writing and editing, and they also require good organizational and decision-making skills—which are certainly necessary for editing and writing jobs.

Education
Give your educational background, listing any degrees and your major or concentration. You may also want to list major courses and/or your thesis title; if you don't have a great deal of work experience in the field, this information may be especially important.

Awards and Honors
List any awards, special recognition, or honors you have received. On the actual résumé you may include all of these or be selective, listing only those specifically related to your chosen career field or those showing significant achievement.

Interests and Hobbies
Sometimes interests and hobbies have a direct bearing on your career goals and should be included in a résumé. They also help round out your presentation of yourself and give prospective employers a more complete idea of your background. But don't use these to the exclusion of information that may be more directly career related.

After writing out this information, you may want to check with close friends and family members to see if you have left out anything of importance. Getting the perspective of others who know you well can be quite helpful in working through this somewhat tedious aspect of résumé writing.

When you're actually writing the résumé, keep in mind that it is essential to use correct grammar. It's wise to consult a few of the many excellent résumé books available when you begin writing your final draft. There you can find many samples of different types of résumés. The Resources section at the end of the chapter includes some recommended books. Many of the job-search books listed at the end of chapter 1 also have helpful résumé sections.

Remember that there is no one correct way to write a résumé: Every employer has different preferences. But these general principles should guide you through résumé preparation. Additionally, you must feel comfortable with the end product; your résumé is about your unique skills and experiences, so use content and a format that presents the unique person you are to best advantage.

TYPES OF RÉSUMÉS

The two basic résumé types are functional and chronological. The chronological résumé organizes work and educational experiences in reverse chronological order (beginning with the most recent and working backward). The standard format lists each employer and job title plus a brief description of the job content. This is most commonly used by people changing positions in the same field.

The functional résumé emphasizes skills and the content or function of previous work, volunteer, or personal experience. This type of résumé is usually used by those who are changing careers and want to emphasize skills they have gained through volunteer work or other experience. Employers often do not like functional résumés because they can obscure work history.

If you like the idea of emphasizing skills and past accomplishments, you could consider using a functional format that includes past employment, usually called a modified functional résumé. The advantage of this type of résumé is that the focus is squarely where it should be—on your demonstrated skills.

INTERNET-SAVVY RÉSUMÉS

Increasingly, résumés are being submitted online through a Web site or sent by e-mail. Additionally, computers are now being used to read résumés by scanning them for key words; you must therefore be certain that your résumé contains the key words that are important for the career you seek (and which, of course, are part of your background). In fact, including a key word or key phrase may be the factor that will land you an interview.

COVER LETTERS

Always include a cover letter with any résumé, whether you are responding to a job advertisement or sending a mailing to many potential employers. A cover letter must be written in correct business style with no grammatical errors and must be produced by typewriter or word processor—never handwritten.

The purpose of a cover letter is to interest an employer in reading your résumé, so it must be interesting and to the point. It must also explain why you're sending your résumé—for example, in response to a job ad, because the organization was recommended to you by someone (give the name if it is a person of influence), or because you are looking for work in this field.

If the letter is in response to an advertised job, focus on your particular skills and experience that relate to this job.

The first paragraph should explain your purpose in sending the résumé. The main body of the letter should briefly describe you and how your unique skills and abilities could fill the employer's needs. Be specific in explaining how you have used your skills to accomplish a certain goal. The closing paragraph should lead to action. You may wish to give a time when you will contact the employer rather than saying that you look forward to hearing from them. You could also state your willingness to send more information.

CREATIVE JOB SEARCH

It is essential to use creativity in your job search and employ many strategies. Apply for jobs listed in newspapers, association or trade publications, and the resources listed in appendix I of this book, but don't let this be the sole focus of your job search.

Also approach personal contacts you may have from summer, volunteer, or part-time jobs. To expand or develop a network of contacts, conduct informational interviews; these can yield information about a career in addition to contacts in the field.

The purpose of an informational interview at this stage of your job search is to ask for advice or suggestions on your job-search strategy. To arrange for an interview, contact someone who is in the career that interests you. Tell this person that you would like some suggestions on your job-search strategy, and ask for a few minutes of his or her time. Bring a list of questions to the interview and conduct yourself very professionally. Ask for names of other people in this field whom you could also contact for helpful information.

Don't ask for a job in this interview, but be prepared with a résumé in case one is requested or a job possibility is mentioned. After the interview, send a letter of thanks, including a résumé if you haven't already left one. You may want to contact these people later in your job search to let them know that you are now looking for a job in the field.

In addition to good job-search information, this strategy yields good contacts in the field. If these contacts were impressed with you during the interview, they may be glad to help you when you let them know you're actively searching for a job. A recommendation from individuals already in this field can be invaluable, because most managers place more faith in the word of people they know than in the actual hiring process.

Through these contacts, you may hear of positions before they are advertised, when there is less competition. Informational interviews will also help you become more comfortable in interview situations; this can yield dividends when you interview for jobs later on.

In addition to consciously working to establish a network by conducting informational interviews, you may locate job possibilities by using the network you already have. Speak with family members, friends, professors, and contacts from part-time, summer, or volunteer work.

Joining the appropriate association and attending its workshops and conferences is another way to network, gain contacts in the field, and learn about job possibilities. Jobs are often listed in association newsletters or journals.

Another strategy for finding jobs is to mail résumés to carefully selected employers. Target organizations or companies that have the type of positions you are seeking, and send your résumé to the appropriate supervisor. Research to obtain this person's name; it's better to direct your résumé to an individual than to a title. Some directories have this information, or the switchboard operator of the company may be able to give you the name. These carefully targeted mailings can lead to interviews, to more networking possibilities, and to actual jobs.

THE JOB INTERVIEW

Many people find the job interview quite frightening. Good preparation should help make this important step in the job-search process much less intimidating. It's also helpful to keep in mind the purpose of the job interview, which is basically for the candidate and the employer to assess each other and decide if this is a good job fit. You probably were invited for an interview because your "paper trail"—your letter and résumé—seemed to fit the qualifications the employer had in mind for this position. Employers interview to make certain a candidate's professional background and work experience match the job that is available. They also want to assess your personality and decide whether you will fit in with the company.

As you prepare for a job interview, try to learn as much as you can about the department in which the opening exists, including its responsibilities and functions. Also try to learn about the work culture of the potential employer (for example, is it rigidly hierarchical with all decisions and initiatives coming from the top, or is there room for individual initiative?) and the personality of the person who would be your supervisor.

This research will help you be more relaxed as you go into the interview. It will also help you formulate questions to obtain more information about the company, evaluate it, and decide whether you want to work for it. Additionally, your knowledge of the employer will be evident in the questions you ask during the interview. The interviewer will be impressed by your research as an indication of your initiative and your desire to work for his or her company.

Before the interview, review your skills and be ready to give specific examples of ways they could benefit the employer. Be prepared for open-ended questions such as, "Tell me about yourself." The employer is not looking for your life history but for pertinent information about you related to the job in question.

Most job-search books include lists of the types of questions generally asked in interviews. It's good to check these out and formulate answers for each one in preparation for the interview.

Don't worry if you're nervous. As you have more interviews, this aspect of job seeking will become more comfortable. Besides, if you are too relaxed, you may not do your best in the interview. Practicing with a friend before the interview can help calm you and prepare you for formulating your thoughts on the spot.

So prepare well for the interview, learn all you can about the employer ahead of time, and review the skills and accomplishments that you will stress in the interview. Then go and do your best. Know realistically that you will not be offered all jobs for which you interview, and likely you will discover that not all of these jobs or employers are quite what you were looking for, either. In addition, competition is keen for many jobs, and many qualified people may have applied. Don't think that not being offered a job reflects negatively on you. Work to maintain your self-confidence during your job search, which may last longer than you anticipate.

Reading about interviews in some of the many books on the market can be helpful as you prepare—but don't build interviewing up to be more difficult than it really is. There is no one right way to interview; as with a résumé, each employer is looking for different things, so what will impress one person won't impress another.

A FINAL WORD

As you go about finding a job, possibly the best advice I can give you is to use more than one strategy. Don't use the Internet to the exclusion of all other methods, for example. And don't neglect the strategy of sending out mass mailings to potential employers. The virtue of these mailings is that the sheer number of letters sent will help you identify employers that have appropriate job openings. The success of this type of job-search campaign is based on a high volume of letters sent. The average response to such a mailing is 2 to 3 percent, so if you mail fewer than 100 letters, you may feel your campaign was a failure.

A mass mailing can be an expensive proposition, but if it yields a job it may be worth the cost. In 1998 the *National Business Employment Weekly* reported on a mass mail campaign in which some twelve hundred letters were mailed out. Within a short period of time twenty-one responses expressing interest were received; eventually three job offers resulted.

If you do decide to send a mass mailing, design it thoughtfully. Carefully target potential employers and aim your letters and résumés to the types of needs these employers would have. Remember to obtain the name of the supervisor in the area where you want to work. This is a lot of work, and it will demand commitment on your part—but it can pay off handsomely.

RESOURCES

Internet

Bolles, Richard Nelson. *Job Hunting on the Internet*. Berkeley, Calif.: Ten Speed Press, 1997.

Crispin, Gerry, and Mark Mehler. *Careerxroads 4th Edition, Career (Cross) Roads: The 1999 Directory to the 500 Best Job, Résumé and Career Management Sites on the World Wide Web* (http://careerxroads.com/).

Kennedy, Joyce Lain, and Thomas J. Morrow. *Electronic Résumé Revolution. Create a Winning Resume for the New World of Job Seeking*. New York: Wiley, 1995.

———. *Electronic Job Search Revolution: How to Win with the New Technology That's Reshaping Today's Job Market*. New York: Wiley, 1995.

Nemnich, Mary B. and Fred E. Jandt. *Cyberspace Résumé Kit: How to Make and Launch a Snazzy Online Résumé*. Indianapolis: JIST Works, 1999.

Oakes, Elizabeth H., ed. *Career Exploration on the Internet: A Student's Guide to More than 300 Web Sites*. Chicago: Ferguson Publishing Company, 1998.

Weddle, Peter D. *Internet Résumés : Take the Net to Your Next Job!* Manassas, Va.: Impact Publications, 1998.

Résumé Books

Enelow, Wendy S. *1500+ Key Words for $100,000+ Jobs*. Manassas, Va.: Impact Publications, 1998.

Infoplace Counseling Staff. *Real World* Résumés. Parma, Ohio: Cuyahoga
County Public Library, 1996.
Krannich, Ronald L. *High Impact* Résumés *and Letters: How to Communicate
Your Qualifications to Employers,* 7th ed. Manassas, Va.: Impact Publica-
tions, 1998.
Krannich, Ronald L., with Caryl Krannich. *Dynamite* Résumés*: 101 Great
Examples and Tips for Success.* Manassas, Va.: Impact Publications, 1999.

Résumé Web Sites
Job Smart Résumé Guide (http://jobsmart.org/tools/resume/index.htm)
Career Mosaic's Résumé Writing Guide (http://www.careermosaic.com/
cm/crc/crc15.html)
What Color Is My Parachute, electronic edition (http://www.washington-
post.com/wp-adv/classi)

Cover Letters
Beatty, Richard H. *The Perfect Cover Letter,* 2d ed. New York: Wiley, 1997.
Krannich, Ronald L., and Caryl Rae Krannich. *201 Dynamite Job Search Let-
ters.* Manassas, Va.: Impact Publications, 1997.
———. *Dynamite Cover Letters: And Other Great Job Search Letters.* Manassas,
Va.: Impact Publications, 1999.

Interviews
Krannich, Ronald L., and Caryl Rae Krannich. *Interview for Success: A Prac-
tical Guide to Increasing Job Interviews, Offers, and Salaries,* 7th ed.
Manassas, Va.: Impact Publications, 1998.
———. *Dynamite Answers to Interview Questions. No More Sweaty Palms!*
Manassas, Va.: Impact Publications, 1999.
———. *Dynamic Networking for Dynamite Jobs.* Manassas, Va.: Impact
Publications, 1996.

General Job-Search Books
Occupational Outlook Handbook 1988-1999. Washington, D.C.: Superinten-
dent of Documents (Bureau of Labor Statistics Bulletin 2500), 1998.
Stoodley, Martha. *Informational Interviewing: How to Tap Your Hidden Job
Market,* 2d ed. Chicago: Ferguson Publishing Company, 1997.
See also the Resources section in chapter 1. Many of these books give infor-
mation about all aspects of the job search.

Appendix I

Job Listings

Job listings can help you find full-time jobs, short-term jobs, and internships. You'll find some listings in the Resources sections in this book; I also give some government listings in appendix III. Following are some additional listings that contain outdoor or outdoor-related careers. Many of these are publications available by subscription; it may be wise to purchase a copy before subscribing to determine if a particular publication will actually help in your search.

Some Internet sites that have job listings are also listed. But I must caution you that Web addresses occasionally change. If you get the dreaded error message after carefully entering the URL for the site, you should first recheck to be certain that you entered the address correctly. If you still get the error message, you may want to conduct your own Web search. Occasionally, however, a Web site is temporarily unavailable while undergoing changes or updating. Another strategy is simply to try again later.

If you have not done so already, consider using some of the resources listed in chapter 10 to locate the most useful Web sites for your needs. Additionally, you might want to recheck the sites of organizations in the field that interest you. Many of these organizations offer some type of job listings or job assistance on their Web sites.

JOBS AVAILABLE

Jobs Available: A Listing of Employment Opportunities in the Public Sector is a bulletin that includes environmental, engineering, conservation, sanitation, and planning positions in addition to other public-sector positions. The western edition includes states from Illinois and Texas west. A yearly subscription is available from:

> *Jobs Available*
> P.O. Box 1040
> Modesto, CA 95353-1040
> Telephone: 209-571-2120
> Fax: 209-576-1249

NATIONAL BUSINESS EMPLOYMENT WEEKLY
National Business Employment Weekly covers jobs available in the United States, and also contains general career articles. It is published by Dow Jones & Company and includes all regional recruitment ads from the *Wall Street Journal.* For subscription information, contact:
> Telephone: 1-800-JOB-HUNT, ext. 205
> Web: http://www.nbew.com/cs/index.htm

CANADA EMPLOYMENT WEEKLY
Canada Employment Weekly covers jobs available in Canada. For subscriptions, contact:
> Mediacorp Canada, Inc.
> 15 Madison Avenue
> Toronto, Ontario M5R 2S2
> Telephone: 416-964-6069
> Fax: 416-964-3202
> Web: http://www.mediacorp2.com/address.html

JOBS IN INTERPRETATION
Members of the National Association of Interpretation receive the newsletter *Jobs in Interpretation* by special request in addition to their other membership benefits. For membership information, contact:
> National Association for Interpretation
> P.O. Box 2246
> Fort Collins, CO 80522
> Telephone: 970-484-8283 or 1-888-900-8283
> Fax: 970-484-8179
> Web: http://www.interpnet.com

JOBSOURCEONLINE.COM
This online resource is useful to both employers and job seekers. It contains a place to post résumés, job listings, and links to other top Internet employment resources. Users also have the option of joining the jobsourceonline.com mailing list.
> Web: http://www.jobsourceonline.com/

THE JOB SEEKER
The Job Seeker is a publication listing jobs in the environmental and natural resources fields. It includes private jobs and jobs with local, state, and the federal government in locations around the country. It contains fairly

complete information about each job and is published twice a month. Subscription rates are available for summer, three months, six months, and one year. Additionally, vacancies that do not get into the newsletter are listed on the Internet. Contact:

The Job Seeker
28672 County EW
Warrens, WI 54666
Telephone and fax: 608-378-4290
Web: http://www.tomah.com/jobseeker

MONSTER.COM
This Web site allows job seekers to post their résumés and research available positions. Employers also use the site to search for candidates. This site is very active; on May 16, 1999, it contained 199,255 job opportunities. Contact:

Telephone: 1-800-MONSTER
Web: http://monster.com

STUDENT CONSERVATION ASSOCIATION (SCA)
A complete listing of internship positions available through SCA can be obtained fro this organization. The positions, which range in length from twelve weeks to twelve months, include travel reimbursement, uniform allowance, housing, and a weekly stipend. The six- to twelve-month positions include, for U.S. citizens, health insurance and an education award. International candidates can apply for twelve- to sixteen-week positions. Contact:

Student Conservation Association, Inc. (SCA)
Recruitment Office
P.O. Box 550
Charlestown, NH 03603
Telephone: 603-543-1700
Fax: 603-543-1828
Web: http://www.sca-inc.org
Web job listings: http://www.sca-inc.org/vol/raca/racanow.htm

ENVIRONMENTAL CAREERS WORLD
Environmental Careers World services were established to recruit top environmental talent for leading environmental consultants, manufacturing industries, government agencies, nongovernmental organizations, and

educational institutions. This group launched the first international environmental job information, recruitment, and career news Web site on Earth Day 1995. Online information includes a job bank, calendar of events, library, education information, and employer services.

The service also publishes the *National Environmental Employment Report*. For a free issue, send your name and mailing address to mailto:ecwo@environmental.com. You can also get subscriptions for various lengths of time. Contact:

> Environmental Careers World
> 100 Bridge Street, Building A
> Hampton, VA 23669
> Telephone: 757-727-7895
> Fax: 757-727-7904
> Web: http://www.environmental-jobs.com/

ENVIRONMENTAL CAREER OPPORTUNITIES (ECO)

This publication contains listings for a great variety of environmental jobs, including advocacy, policy, conservation, and internship positions. The Web site contains a sampling of the jobs available through the print publication, which is published every two weeks and bills itself as "the only comprehensive source of job listings in the environmental field." To subscribe, contact:

> Brubach Publishing Company, Inc.
> HCR 4, Box 65
> Leon, VA 22725
> Telephone: 1-800-315-9777
> Fax: 804-985-2331
> E-mail: ecojobs@mindspring.com
> Web: http://www.ecojobs.com

MORE INTERNET SITES

For jobs in the United States (http://www.jobbankusa.com/)
For jobs in Canada (http://www.canadajobs.com/)
Ubiquity Environmental Careers Page:
> (http://ourworld.compuserve.com/homepages/ubikk/)

Appendix II

United States and Canadian Sources of Labor Market Information

For detailed labor market reports covering current and future employment in a particular state, you can contact the chief of labor research and analysis in that state or province. Below is a listing of titles and addresses.

This listing also includes Internet addresses, when available. A word of caution, however: Internet addresses do change. If the address given does not produce the Web site, try a search using both the state or province and department names. Additionally, the Web sites vary tremendously in the type of information they give. Some have absolutely no labor force information. Others have job listings, statistics, and other useful information for job researchers and job seekers. Most likely the quality of state Web pages will improve in the years to come as Internet use increases. And those states with no Web page at this time will likely develop sites shortly.

UNITED STATES

Alabama

Chief, Research and Statistics
Department of Industrial Relations
Industrial Relations Building
649 Monroe Street
Montgomery, AL 36131
Web: http://129.66.172.4/dir/index.html

Alaska

Chief, Research and Analysis
Employment Security Division
Department of Labor
P.O. Box 25509
Juneau, AK 99802-5509
Web: http://www.state.ak.us/local/akpages/LABOR/home.htm

Arizona

Chief, Labor Market Information
Research and Analysis
Department of Economic Security
P.O. Box 6123
Phoenix, AZ 85005
Web: http://www.state.az.us/gv/dept/des.html

Arkansas

Chief, Research and Statistics
Employment Security Division
2 Capitol Mall, Rm. 61
Little Rock, AR 72201
Web: http://www.state.ar.us/esd/ark-esd.html

California

Chief, Workforce Development Office
Employment Development Department
P.O. Box 826880
Sacramento, CA 94280-0001
Web: http://www.calmis.cahwnet.gov/

Colorado

Chief, Labor Market Information Office
Department of Labor and Employment
1515 Arapahoe Street, Tower 2, Suite 300
Denver, CO 80202-2117
Web: http://www.state.co.us/gov_dir/labor_dir/labor_home.html

Connecticut

Director, Research and Information
Labor Department
200 Folly Brook Boulevard
Wethersfield, CT 06109
Web: http://www.ctdol.state.ct.us/lmi/index.htm

Delaware

Chief, Occupational and Labor Market Information Office
Department of Labor
4425 North Market Street
Wilmington, DE 19802
Web: http://www.oolmi.net/soicc/oolmi_soicc_default.asp

District of Columbia

Employment Services Department
500 C Street, NW, Suite 600
Washington, DC 20001
Web:http://www.ci.washington.dc.us/employment_opportunities.html

Florida

Chief, Research and Statistics
Department of Labor and Employment
2012 Capitol Circle Southeast, Hartman Building
Tallahassee, FL 32399-2152
Web: http://sun6.dms.state.fl.us/dles/

Georgia

Director, Information Systems
Department of Labor
148 International Boulevard Northeast, Suite 600
Atlanta, GA 30303
Web: http://www.dol.state.ga.us/

Hawaii

Chief, Research and Statistics Directorate
Department of Labor and Industrial Relations
830 Punchbowl Suite, Room 321
Honolulu, HI 96813
Web: http://www.aloha.net/~edpso/

Idaho

Chief, Research and Analysis
Department of Employment
317 Main Street
Boise, ID 83735

Illinois

Manager, Research and Analysis Division
Department of Employment Security
401 South State Street
Chicago, IL 60605
Web: http://il.jobsearch.org/

Indiana

Chief, Research
Employment Standards Division
Department of Labor
100 North Senate Avenue, Room 1013
Indianapolis, IN 46204
Web: http://www.ai.org/labor/index.html

Iowa

Workforce Development Department
1000 East Grand Avenue
Des Moines, IA 50319-0209
Web: http://www.state.ia.us/government/wd/index.htm

Kansas

Chief, Research and Analysis
Department of Human Resources
401 Soutwest Topeka Boulevard
Topeka, KS 66603-3182
Web: http://www.ink.org/public/kdhr/

Kentucky

Chief, Workforce Analysis and Research
Workforce Development Cabinet
Capital Plaza Tower
500 Mero Street, Second Floor
Frankfort, KY 40601
Web: http://www.state.ky.us/agencies/wforce/index.htm

Louisiana

Chief, Research and Statistics
Office of Employment Security
Labor Department
P.O. Box 94094
Baton Rouge, LA 70804-9094
Web: http://www.ldol.state.la.us/

Maine

Director, Labor Market Information Services
Labor Department
20 Union Street, P.O. Box 309
Augusta, ME 04332-0309

Maryland

Director, Research and Analysis
Department of Human Resources
311 West Saratoga Street
Baltimore, MD 21201
Web: http://www.gl.umbc.edu/~hickman/dhr2.html

Massachusetts

Director, Employment and Training Division
Labor and Workforce Development Department
Hurley Building, Government Center
Boston, MA 02114

Michigan

Director, Research and Statistics Division
Employment Security Commission
7310 Woodward Avenue
Detroit, MI 48202

Minnesota

Director, Research and Statistical Office
Economic Security Department
390 North Robert Street
St. Paul, MN 55101
Web: http://www.des.state.mn.us/

Mississippi

Chief, Research and Statistics
Employment Security Commission
P.O. Box 1699
Jackson, MS 39215

Missouri

Chief, Research and Statistics
Division of Employment Security
Department of Labor and Industrial Relations
421 East Dunklin Street
Jefferson City, MO 65104-0059
Web: http://www.dolir.state.mo.us/

Montana

Chief, Research and Analysis
Department of Labor and Industry
P.O. Box 1728
Helena, MT 59624

Nebraska

Chief, Research and Statistics
Labor Market Information Section
Department of Labor
P.O. Box 94600
Lincoln, NE 68509-4600
Web: http://www.dol.state.ne.us/

Nevada

Chief, Employment Security Research
Employment Security Department
500 East Third Street
Carson City, NV 89713

New Hampshire
Director, Economic Analysis and Reports
Department of Employment Security
32 South Main Street
Concord, NH 03301-4857
Web: http://www.nhworks.state.nh.us/

New Jersey
Director, Labor Research and Analysis
Department of Labor
P.O. Box 056
Trenton, NJ 08625-0110
Web: http://www.state.nj.us/labor/

New Mexico
Chief, Research and Statistics
Employment Security Division
Department of Labor
P.O. Box 1928
Albuquerque, NM 87103
Web: http://www3.state.nm.us/dol/dol_lmif.html

New York
Director, Division of Research and Statistics
Department of Labor
State Campus, Building 12
Albany, NY 12240
Web: http://www.labor.state.ny.us/

North Carolina
Director, Public Information
Department of Labor
4 West Edenton Street
Raleigh, NC 27601
Web: http://www.dol.state.nc.us/DOL/

North Dakota

Chief, Research and Statistics
Job Service
P.O. Box 5507
Bismarck, ND 58506-5507
Web: http://www.state.nd.us/jsnd/lmi.htm

Ohio

Director, Labor Market Information
Bureau of Employment Services
P.O. Box 1618
Columbus, OH 43216-1618
Web: http://www.ohio.gov/obes/

Oklahoma

Chief, Research and Planning Division
Employment Security Commission
P.O. Box 52009
Oklahoma City, OK 73105-2003
Web: http://www.oesc.state.ok.us/

Oregon

Assistant Administrator, Research and Statistics
Bureau of Labor and Industries
800 Northeast Oregon Street
Portland, OR 97232

Pennsylvania

Director, Research and Statistics Bureau
Department of Labor and Industry
1700 Labor and Industry Building
Harrisburg, PA 17120
Web: http://www.li.state.pa.us/

Rhode Island

Labor Market Information and Management Services
Labor and Training Department
101 Friendship Street
Providence, RI 02903
Web: http://www.state.ri.us/stdept/sd33.htm

South Carolina

Director, Labor Market Information
Employment Security Commission
P.O. Box 995
Columbia, SC 29202
Web: http://scjob.sces.org/

South Dakota

Chief, Research and Statistics
Labor and Management Division
Department of Labor
700 Governors Drive
Pierre, SD 57501
Web: http://www.state.sd.us/state/executive/dol/dol.htm

Tennessee

Chief, Research and Statistics
Department of Employment Security
12th Floor, Davey Crockett Tower
Nashville, TN 37245-0001
Web: http://www.state.tn.us/employsecurity/

Texas

Chief, Economic Research and Analysis
Workforce Commission
101 East 15th Street
Austin, TX 78778
Web: http://www.twc.state.tx.us/

Utah

Director, Research and Analysis
Labor Commission
Department of Employment Security
P.O. Box 11249
Salt Lake City, UT 84147
Web: http://www.ind-com.state.ut.us/

Vermont

Chief, Research and Statistics
Employment and Training Department
P.O. Box 488, 5 Green Mountain Drive
Montpelier, VT 05601-0488
Web: http://www.det.state.vt.us/

Virginia

Commissioner
Virginia Employment Commission
703 East Main Street
Richmond, VA 23219
Web: http://www.vec.state.va.us/

Washington

Chief, Research and Statistics
Employment Security Department
P.O. Box 9046
Olympia, WA 98507-9046
Web: http://www.wa.gov/esd/

West Virginia

Chief, Employment Services Division
Bureau of Employment Programs
112 California Avenue
Charleston, WV 25305
Web: http://www.state.wv.us/bep/lmi/default.htm

Wisconsin

Labor & Industry Review Commission
P.O. Box 8126
Madison, WI 53708

Wyoming

Chief, Research and Analysis
Department of Employment
Herschler Building, Second Floor East
122 West 25th Street
Cheyenne, WY 82002
Web: http://www.state.wy.us/state/
government/state_agencies/text-employment.html

Puerto Rico

Chief, Research and Statistics
Labor and Human Research Department
505 Munoz-Rivera Avenue, 21st Floor
Hato Rey, PR 00918

CANADA

This national government department maintains a Web site that contains general information for the country and links to specific information for all provinces and territories. Particularly useful is the mega site (http://lmi-imt.hrdc-drhc.gc.ca/owa_lmi/owa/sp_show_lmi?l=e&i=1).

Human Resources Development Canada
Place du Portage, Phase IV
140 Promenade du Portage
Hull, Quebec K1A 0J9
Telephone: 819-994-2482
Web: http://www.hrdc-drhc.gc.ca/common/lmi.shtml

Office of the Minister of Labour
Place du Portage, Phase II
165 Hotel de Ville Street, 11th Floor
Hull, Quebec K1A 0J2
Telephone: 819-953-5646
Fax: 819-994-5168
Web: http://labour-travail.hrdc-drhc.gc.ca/main.cfm

Appendix III

Government Employment

Many outdoor jobs can be found with various branches of the U.S. federal government or with other national governments, such as the government of Canada. Some of these branches or departments are listed in earlier chapters in this book, especially when they are primary employers for certain types of careers.

If you wish to work for the Canadian or U.S. national government, you will find it to your advantage to first gain some understanding of the federal employment system. The Resources section of this appendix gives a Web site that lists jobs with the Canadian government and gives details about applying for these jobs. You may also find helpful data in the labor market information Web sites for Canada, listed in the appendix II.

During the 1990s the U.S. federal government employment system changed; some changes were still being implemented at the time of writing. These included allowing more freedom to agencies in recruiting employees, and changing the way federal salaries are weighed against jobs in the private sector. To understand the system currently in effect, you should contact the U.S. Office of Personnel Management (OPM), which serves as the personnel agency for the government. You can obtain the telephone number from the government pages in your local telephone directory, or you can get details from the OPM Web site listed in the Resources section of this appendix.

One prominent trend in the United States in the 1990s was a reduction in the size of the federal government; in fact, more than two hundred thousand federal jobs were eliminated. Only a small proportion of those losing their jobs actually left involuntarily, however; many left because of job buyouts or retirements. And the U.S. federal government is still hiring employees. For example, in 1995 some forty-four thousand new employees were hired, which made the federal government the most active employer in the country in terms of new hires for that year.

The OPM regulates civil service requirements, which include selection and advancement on the basis of merit; recruitment from all segments of society; and fair treatment without regard to differences of politics, race, color, national origin, religion, sex, marital status, age, or handicap. Constitutional rights and individual privacy are guaranteed, as are equal pay for work of equal value and high standards of integrity and conduct. The OPM is also involved with formulating policies and ensuring compliance with federal personnel regulations.

Another way to get a job with the government is to go directly to the nearest office of the agency that interests you. Each agency posts a listing of internal vacancies available, and this is where the hiring takes place. If you locate a job that interests you and you meet the requirements, you can submit an application directly to the agency. If you have previously filed a résumé with the OPM, you can request that the OPM consider your application for that position.

Competition is usually very keen for federal jobs, and if you are really interested in working for the government, it is worth taking the time to ensure that your application receives full consideration. When you submit your résumé, take care to target your qualifications to the specifications for this job. Alternately, you may complete the two-page Federal Employment OF-612.

Obtaining jobs with the U.S. federal government can be a difficult and time-consuming process. If working for the federal government is your goal, however, time spent researching the federal occupational classification system and learning how to write a résumé that shows off your qualifications will help you reach this goal. Check out some of the excellent books about working for the government, such as those in the Resources section of this appendix.

RESOURCES

Federal Career Opportunities
The print edition of this biweekly, private publication lists more than four thousand jobs; the online version lists more than eleven thousand. Contact:

> *Federal Career Opportunities*
> Federal Research Service, Inc.
> P.O. Box 1059
> Vienna, VA 22183-1059
> Telephone: 1-800-822-5627
> Web: http://www.fedjobs.com

Jobs Available: A Listing of Employment Opportunities in the Public Sector
See appendix I for information on this publication.

USA Jobs by Phone

Telephone: 912-757-3000; follow instructions to obtain current job openings, general information on federal employment policies and procedures, and "what's hot."

Internet Sites

Jobs with the U.S. government and other information about applying for U.S. government jobs are available at this Office of Personnel Management site (http://www.usajobs.opm.gov/)

Jobs with the Canadian government and job application information can be located at this Human Resources Development Canada site: (http://ele.ingenia.com/)

Books

Lauber, Daniel, ed. *Government Job Finder*, 3d ed. River Forest, Ill.: Planning Communications (7215 Oak Avenue, 60305), 1997.

Smith, Russ. *Federal Jobs in Law Enforcement*. Manassas Park, Va.: Impact Press, 1996.

Troutman, Kathryn K. *Reinvention: Federal Résumés*. Washington, D.C.: The Résumé Place (1725 K Street, NW, 20006), 1997. Also available is a PC disk that contains five résumés.

Index

Birkby, Bob, xv
  on writing and trail building, 170–72
Botanical Society of America, 39
botany, 26–30
  plant exploration, 27–28
  plant pathology, 28–29
  plant physiology, 29–30
  plant taxonomy, 26–27
  resource, 39
  resource management, 30
Bradshaw, Bill, on fisheries biology, 73–75
Brubach Publishing Company, Inc., 186
bull riding, professional, xvii

Calvert, Robert, Jr., foreword by, ix–x
camping careers, 131–32
  resources, 143–44
Canada Employment Weekly, 184
Canadian Camping Association, 144
Canadian Council of Professional
  Engineers, 105
The Canadian Federation of Agriculture, 18
Canadian Forest Service, 68
Canadian Meteorological and
  Oceanographic Society, 89
Canadian Museums Association, 165
Canadian Nature Federation, 65
Canadian Parks and Recreation
  Association, 144
Canadian Veterinary Medical Association, 40
Canadian Wildlife Service, 67
Career (Cross) Roads (Crispin and Mehler),
  181
career counselors, 4–5
Career Exploration on the Internet
  (Oakes, ed.), 181
career information, xvii–xviii
The Career Interests Game, 6
Career Mosaic's Resume Writing Guide, 182
*Career Planning and Job Searching in the
  Information Age* (Lorensen,ed.), 6
career selection, 1
  books, 5–6
  interests, 2
  Internet as resource, 5
  personality and temperament, 4
  resources, 4–6
  skills, 2–3
  values, 3
  web sites, 6
  working in career setting, 4
  see also job-search tips
cartographers, 82
Cat Tales Zoological Park, 34

Training Center, 41
Center for Museum Studies, 165
ceramic engineering, 95
Change Your Job (Krannich and Krannich), 6
chemical engineering, 95
civil engineering, 95, 97
  profile, 107–8
  resource, 105
College of Oceaneering, 124–25
Colorado School of Mines, 106
commercial shipping industry. *See*
  merchant marine
Commins, Michael, on ski patrolling, 148–50
conservation, 51–52
  careers, 52–65
  profiles, 71–79
  resources, 65–70
  seasonal and volunteer work in, 64–65
  web sites, 70
Conservation Directory, 1999, 164
conservation district work, 59–60
conservation and environmental
  organization work, 161–63
  resources, 164
Cool Works, 70, 146
cover letters, 177–78
  resources, 182
crop science, 8
Crop Science Society of America, 16
cruise ship positions, 134–36
  crew, 134, 135–36
  resources, 144–45
  staff, 134, 135
Cyber-Sierra's Natural Resources Job
  Search, 70
Cyberspace Résumé Kit (Nemnich and
  Jandt), 181

Dawson, Phyllis, on horse industry
  careers, 146–48
Discover the Best Jobs for You (Krannich
  and Krannich), 6
diving, commercial, 122–24
  profile, 128–29
  resources, 124–25
diving instruction, 136–37
  resources, 144
Doing Work You Love (Gilman), 6
Dynamic Networking for Dynamite Jobs
  (Krannich and Krannich), 182
Dynamite Answers to Interview Questions
  (Krannich and Krannich), 182
Dynamite Cover Letters (Krannich and
  Krannich), 182

SOUTHEASTERN COMMUNITY COLLEGE LIBRARY

3 3255 00064 5573